D1261484

Josephine Herbst

Twayne's United States Authors Series

Kenneth Eble, Editor
University of Utah

TUSAS 468

JOSEPHINE HERBST
1892–1969
Photograph reproduced from New Green World *(1954),*
Hastings House, Publishers, Inc., New York

Josephine Herbst

By Winifred Farrant Bevilacqua

University of Turin

Twayne Publishers • Boston

for Nicola

Josephine Herbst

Winifred Farrant Bevilacqua

Copyright © 1985 by G.K. Hall & Company
All Rights Reserved
Published by Twayne Publishers
A Division of G. K. Hall & Co.
A publishing subsidiary of ITT
70 Lincoln Street
Boston, Massachusetts 02111

Book Production by Lyda Kuth
Book Design by Barbara Anderson

Printed on permanent/durable acid-free
paper and bound in the United States of America.

Library of Congress Cataloging in Publication Data

Bevilacqua, Winifred Farrant, 1947–
  Josephine Herbst.
(Twayne's United States authors series; TUSAS 468)
Bibliography: p. 120
Includes index.
  1. Herbst, Josephine, 1897–1969—Criticism and interpretation.
I. Title. II. Series.
PS3515.E596Z58 1985   813'.52   84-19230
ISBN 0-8057-7409-2

Contents

About the Author

Winifred Farrant Bevilacqua is lecturer in American Literature at the University of Turin, Italy. A graduate of Seton Hall University, she received her M.A. and Ph.D. degrees from the University of Iowa and her D.Litt. from the University of Milan, Italy. She edited *Fiction by American Women: Recent Views* (Port Washington, N.Y.: Associated Faculty Press, 1983).

Preface

As a writer whose work comprises almost half a century of faithful witness to many central realities of American life and always offers a challenging commentary on general human problems, Josephine Herbst should be accorded attention commensurate with her accomplishments. She made her literary debut in the 1920s with novels and stories that earned her a reputation as a promising new talent. During the 1930s, when she wrote a trilogy in the vein of the politically and socially oriented panoramic fiction typical of those years and fulfilled challenging assignments as a journalist reporting on agrarian crises in the United States and on social upheaval abroad, she was regarded as a major figure in the radical movement in American literature. Although she experienced a crisis in her art in the 1940s, when she published her last two novels, from the early 1950s until her death in 1969 she explored with versatility various types of literary expression, producing a biography, a novella, and several insightful memoirs about the artistic and political life of the years between the two world wars.

The present study intends to be a balanced assessment of Herbst's most important writings. After a first chapter that offers a brief profile of her life and a second that considers the consistent structural and stylistic characteristics of her narrative, the following three take up in chronological order all of her published novels, allotting to each a more or less extended discussion. Her shorter fictional works, as well as her biography of John and William Bartram, are the subject of chapter 6. Devoted to Herbst as a social and cultural commentator, chapter 7 focuses on her memoirs and her 1930s journalism. The last chapter provides summary remarks on her significance as a literary figure. The underlying premise of this book is that Josephine Herbst, once better known, will richly reward continued study by a new generation of readers and critics.

Winifred Farrant Bevilacqua

University of Turin

Acknowledgments

Permission to quote from the following works by Josephine Herbst has been granted by Georges Borchardt, Inc.:

Rope of Gold. New York: Harcourt, Brace & Co., 1939.
Satan's Sergeants. New York: Charles Scribner's Sons, 1941.
Somewhere the Tempest Fell. New York: Charles Scribner's Sons, 1947.
"Hunter of Doves." *Botteghe Oscure* 3 (Spring 1954).
"The Ruins of Memory." *Nation* 182 (April 14, 1956).
"Nathanael West." *Kenyon Review* 23 (Fall 1961).
"The Starched Blue Sky of Spain." *Noble Savage* 1 (March 1960).
"A Year of Disgrace." *Noble Savage* 3 (May 1961).
"Yesterday's Road." *New American Review* 3 (April 1968).

Chronology

1892	Josephine Herbst born on March 5 in Sioux City, Iowa, to William Benton Herbst and Mary Frey Herbst.
1910	Graduates from high school in Sioux City.
1910–1912	Attends Morningside College in Sioux City.
1912–1913	Studies at the University of Iowa, Iowa City, Iowa.
1913–1914	Teaches school in Stratford, Iowa.
1915–1916	Does secretarial work for a law firm in Seattle, Washington, and is a part-time student at the University of Washington.
1917	Attends the University of California at Berkeley; publishes several poems in the *Occident,* the student literary magazine.
1918	Receives bachelor of arts degree in English from Berkeley.
1919–1922	Moves to New York City and associates with members of radical literary and political circles; after holding a number of odd jobs, becomes a reader for the *Smart Set.*
1922–1924	Lives in Germany and Italy, then spends time with the expatriate writers in Paris where she meets John Herrmann; completes her first novel, "Following the Circle," never to be published.
1925	Moves to New Preston, Connecticut.
1926–1927	Marries John Herrmann on September 2, 1926; lives in New York City where she and Herrmann participate in the life of the literary community in Greenwich Village. Is disillusioned by the execution of Sacco and Vanzetti.
1928	*Nothing Is Sacred,* a novel. Settles in Erwinna, Pennsylvania, in the house which is to be her home for the next forty years.
1929	*Money for Love,* a novel.

1930   Goes to Russia; she and Herrmann visit Moscow and, in November, attend the Second World Plenum of the Bureau of Revolutionary Literature in Kharkov.

1932–1934   Travels in the Midwest to report on the agrarian situation for *Scribner's Magazine* (1933), *New Masses* (1934), and the *American Mercury* (1935).

1933   *Pity Is Not Enough,* first volume of a trilogy.

1934   *The Executioner Waits,* second volume of the trilogy.

1935   Writes about a general strike in Cuba for *New Masses;* reports from Germany on the Nazi regime for the *New York Post* and the *Nation; Post* articles reprinted in pamphlet form by the Anti-Nazi Federation. Separates from John Herrmann.

1936   Receives a Guggenheim Award in the field of the novel.

1937   Goes to Spain to report on the Spanish Civil War; is one of the few women journalists allowed to visit the front lines.

1939   *Rope of Gold* concludes trilogy. Journeys in several South American countries.

1940   Divorces John Herrmann.

1941   *Satan's Sergeants,* a novel.

1942   Obtains a job as an antiwar propagandist for the Coordinator of Information in Washington, D.C.; a few months later, is dismissed from that job. Moves to Chicago where she works for the Public Health Service and reviews books for the Chicago *Sun.*

1944   Returns to Erwinna, Pennsylvania.

1947   *Somewhere the Tempest Fell,* a novel.

1954   *New Green World,* a biography. "Hunter of Doves," a novella, in *Botteghe Oscure.*

1956   "The Ruins of Memory," a retrospective essay on the 1920s and the 1930s, in the *Nation.*

1958   Holds a fellowship at the Newberry Library.

1960   "The Starched Blue Sky of Spain," the first of her memoirs, for which she receives the Longview Foundation Award for Non-fiction in 1961, appears in the *Noble Savage*.

1961   "A Year of Disgrace," a memoir, in the *Noble Savage*.

1962–1963   Visits various European countries.

1965   Receives a Rockefeller Foundation Grant for work on her memoirs.

1966   Recipient of a grant from the National Institute of Arts and Letters.

1967   National Book Awards judge with Granville Hicks and John Updike.

1968   "Yesterday's Road," a memoir, in *New American Review*. Establishes an archive of personal papers in the Collection of American Literature, the Beinecke Rare Book and Manuscript Library, Yale University.

1969   Dies in New York City on January 28.

Chapter One
To Meet the Writer

Josephine Herbst, the third of four sisters, was born in Sioux City, Iowa, on March 5, 1892, several years after her parents, of German and Swiss origin, had come to Iowa from Emmaus, Pennsylvania, in search of a better life. Her father, William Herbst, sold farm implements in northwest Iowa, Nebraska, and the Dakotas, but his business, which never flourished and eventually failed, did not allow the family more than a modest living. As a child, Herbst recalled:

I drove all over this country with my father, eating fried chicken and chewing corn on the cob, and when the crops were in he and I would take the team and drive around to see what cash we could pick up on old debts. . . . Land prices soared during those years. Yet he went out burdened with the outlawed debts of farmers who year after year didn't have cash to meet their payments.[1]

Her mother, Mary, was an energetic and imaginative woman who never managed to get accustomed to rural Iowa and always spoke with enthusiasm about life "back East." A fine storyteller, she played an important role in stimulating the interest in writing that her daughter displayed from early youth.

In a family of omnivorous readers, Josephine was the most avid. During hot summer days, she remembered, she experienced "muscular enervation . . . accompanied by a curious mental excitement that required countless books from the library, read in what approached a state of trance."[2] Her youthful literary fare included *The Pilgrim's Progress, The Way of All Flesh,* and *Madame Bovary,* as well as copies of the journal *The Appeal to Reason.* Reportedly, while still a schoolgirl, she had a story printed in the local newspaper.

Upon completing high school in 1910, Herbst entered Morningside College in Sioux City to study literature. But her home town had never satisfied her personal and intellectual needs and so, after two years, she transferred to the University of Iowa in Iowa City. Financial problems at home forced her to interrupt her studies in the summer of 1913 and her occupations over the next four years would respectively be: teaching elementary school in Stratford, Iowa; holding a clerical job in Sioux City; working in a law office in Seattle while taking a few courses at the University of Washington; again being a secretary in her home town. By the summer of 1917 she had enough money to resume her education and chose to spend her last year of college at the University of California at Berkeley. There she published a handful of poems in the *Occident,* the student literary magazine, and began to manifest radical sentiments by actively sympathizing with antiwar movements on campus.

After she received her Bachelor of Arts in English in 1918, she worked as a secretary in the San Francisco area and in Seattle. In October 1919 she moved to New York. Having already decided on writing as a career, she supported herself and enlarged her experience by working at a variety of jobs, including clerking in a department store and doing case work for a charitable organization. Only later on did she find relevant employment, as an editorial reader for the *Smart Set,* a national magazine then edited by H. L. Mencken and George Jean Nathan. Her first short stories, "The Elegant Mr. Gason" and "Happy Birthday!" were to appear in this magazine under her pseudonym, Carlotta Greet. While in New York, Herbst also began to form friendships with artists and writers who encouraged her growing awareness both of social problems and of literary currents. The most congenial of these friends were Genevieve Taggard, Albert Rhys Williams, Michael Gold, and Floyd Dell, a lively group associated with the *Masses* and the *Liberator.* It was at this time that she had an affair with the young playwright Maxwell Anderson, which ended badly in the summer of 1920 when she reluctantly agreed to terminate an unexpected pregnancy.[3] Her unhappiness over this experience was soon sharpened by the death of her beloved younger sister Helen.

In May 1922, following the lead of the aspiring writers of her generation, she sailed for Europe. Of this move she later wrote:

In the 1920's no one had to give a rational explanation for going to Europe; mobility was in the blood. The Great War had moved all adventuring, all romance to Europe; in America . . . the artist was . . . an "outsider." . . . The great love affair for the American youth of the 1920s was. a love affair with the world. To get out of the constricting present, away from Puritanism, prohibition, away from the groveling role of "outsider," of indifferent victor, of a creditor nation in a world in distress. That youthful generation *knew* that the old world was gone forever; that the apparent stability and material progress of society had rested, like everything else human, upon the void. But in America the pretense was that nothing had changed. To get in the vortex, to face up to the stern reality may become an urge, a passionate need, and instinctively, knowingly, the young artists determined to submit to it. It was more a desire to *feel* what was in the world to be felt, than to escape something, in America, that impelled the youth of that decade to make their pilgrimage.[4]

After visiting friends in London and traveling on the continent, she settled in Berlin. Her recollections of Germany in her memoir "Yesterday's Road" stress her attempts to immerse herself in German life and how these experiences intensified her interest in social ills and radical solutions:

I had dissolved among Germans in the inflation days of 1923; when I had mingled with the rich in swank hotels or nibbled ersatz cakes with uneasy bourgeoisie in a pleasant pension of Kastanienalle . . . or shared black bread and cabbage with students in their unheated Studentheim in Marburg . . . or paid ten cents to take a train to Dresden to hear the opera . . . or revelled at a different theater every night where needy Germans strained to spend their paper marks before tomorrow made them trash . . . Then I . . . forsook this intoxicating realm . . . and dived down and for months lived cheek by jowl with the poor in gloomy tenements of Moabit and Wedding. And you can say that the poor won out.[5]

Her time, however, was also absorbed by work on "Following the Circle," a novel she was later to complete but never to publish. As would be her practice in most of her fiction, in developing this book Herbst drew on personal experience. The death of her sister Helen and her affair with Maxwell Anderson are, in fact, the two events around which the story is built. At the end of her stay in Germany in the fall of 1923, she moved to Italy and lodged for several months in a pension in Florence.

The following spring she went to Paris, the meeting ground for the literary expatriates of the 1920s. There she socialized with many of the young artists of the Left Bank and established lasting friendships with Ernest Hemingway, Nathan Asch, and Robert McAlmon. She also fell in love with her future husband, John Herrmann, a native of Michigan who had studied art history in Munich and was determined to become a serious writer. Herbst and Herrmann plunged into the heady atmosphere of the city and made the rounds of the sidewalk cafés and literary ateliers where other young intellectuals from middle America talked about art, literature, and life. Herrmann was very enthusiastic about all kinds of experimental writing and was delighted when one of his short pieces, entitled simply "Work in Progress," appeared in Robert McAlmon's *The Contact Collection of*

Contemporary Writing. By contrast, although she may have been influenced by Hemingway's method of writing, Herbst managed in general to maintain a philosophic distance from "the lost generation."

By the fall of 1924 she was back in New York with Herrmann, whom she was to marry in September 1926. After a period spent caring for her ailing mother in Sioux City, she and Herrmann went to live in an old farmhouse in New Preston, Connecticut, where they immersed themselves in literature and followed a rigid schedule of reading and writing. She was working on *Nothing Is Sacred,* a novel based on her most recent experiences in Sioux City, and he was busy with "Engagement," a novelette critical of the middle class that would be printed in *The Second American Caravan* (1928). In a short time, with the arrival of people like Katherine Anne Porter and her husband Ernest Stock, Nathan Asch and his wife, New Preston became a sort of informal artists' colony.

Returning to New York in September 1926, the Herrmanns brought with them their manuscripts and a good deal of optimism. Although it would take two years before their works were published, as Herbst once remarked, "In the twenties a young writer expected a run-around for a first venture. But no one waited for a first novel 'to be taken' before beginning new work. Now it was only a question of what next."[6] To earn money, Herrmann sold books at Brentano's store and Herbst first researched working conditions in New York laundries and then did editorial work for the publishing houses Vanguard Press and Dell. Their tight financial situation, she would observe, was not unusual, for "if the country was in high-gear prosperity, none of the young people we knew were sharing it."[7] In fact, their friends Allen Tate and Caroline Gordon shared a basement apartment rent-free in exchange for janitorial services, while Katherine Anne Porter lived in a rickety building its tenants referred to as "Casa Caligari."

Nothing Is Sacred, finally published in the fall of 1928, received generally favorable reviews. By that time the Herrmanns were living in Bucks County, Pennsylvania, in an old stone house they had persuaded his wealthy parents to purchase for them. For Herbst, who would make her home there for the rest of her life, this move meant a return to her origins, since Erwinna, the site of their house, was just fifteen miles from the Old Blue Church at Emmaus where her ancestors were buried. Their decision to live in the country, she later maintained, was not made in revolt against city life: "We weren't in love with the soil per se . . . We loved the outdoors but we liked the city also. But to stay in the city meant harnessing yourself to a regular job so that you could pay rent."[8] Working steadily in Erwinna, she wrote *Money for Love,* a novel about young drifters in New York, which when it appeared in 1929 was not so highly praised as *Nothing Is Sacred.*

At the suggestion of Michael Gold, in the fall of 1930 Herbst and Herrmann went to Russia as unofficial delegates to a writers' congress. Their trip to Russia was timely. With the collapse of the stock market and the onset of the Depression, for a growing number of intellectuals the example of the Soviet Union seemed to provide an alternative to democratic capitalism and a plausible replacement for the dying American dream. And so, eager to see the land in which socialism was already in operation, many made their pilgrimage to Russia. The Herrmanns arrived in Moscow in October, 1930 and the next month attended the Second World Plenum of the International Bureau of Revolutionary Literature held in Kharkov. Herbst's mixed reactions to what she learned at the congress were reflected in an article she wrote for the *New Republic* where, after thoughtfully evaluating the debate about the creation of a new social literature, she voiced her fears concerning the fate of the writer in a nation undergoing a revolution.

There is no time in the Soviet Union for literature in the old meaning of the term. A too critical writer may endanger the state and he is silenced. The writer is a part of life; he is a political atom as well as a literary one. He lives in a wartime atmosphere and the country has taken the attitude all wartime countries take, of suppressing the dissenting voices. Nothing much comes out of a country during war, and nothing much in the way of literature, as we are accustomed to think of it, can come out of the Soviet Union.[9]

By the time they returned home, it was clear to everyone that the United States was experiencing the most devastating depression of its history. Responding to the crushing necessities of the period, many writers were abandoning the "aestheticism" that had characterized their work during the 1920s and were turning their attention to problems of a social and political nature. This change in content was often accompanied by a new awareness of social philosophies, particularly of Marxist ideology. Josephine Herbst's prior work had not been entirely void of social criticism but now she too decided to direct her fictional interests toward the pressing issues of the day. To this end, she reworked her plans for a fictionalized version of her family's history into a reinterpretation of the development of American society from the time of the Civil War through the Depression. The result was to be a trilogy, *Pity Is Not Enough* (1933), *The Executioner Waits* (1934), and *Rope of Gold* (1939), three works intended to cover "not only the decay of capitalistic society, but also the upthrust of a new group society."[10]

Owing to the gravity of the crisis, most members of the American intellectual community also felt that they could no longer keep themselves aloof from active sociopolitical involvement. Herbst was no exception. Indeed, few writers of the 1930s reflected more directly than she the interaction of art and ideology since along with writing her trilogy she undertook a series of challenging journalistic assignments related to economic and political struggles at home and abroad.

For *New Masses* she analyzed the notorious Scottsboro trial, at the end of which nine young black men were summarily sentenced to death for the rape of two white women. Her article, "Lynching in the Quiet Manner," links the case to the general conditions of Southern blacks at that time and deplores the fact that the National Association for the Advancement of Colored People, on the grounds that the incident was being exploited as Communist propaganda, had refused to aid the defendants. Also in 1931, along with Theodore Dreiser, Sherwood Anderson, and John Dos Passos, she became a member of the National Committee for the Defense of Political Prisoners.

During the next few years Herbst took several trips to the Midwest to gather material for articles on agrarian problems. In 1932 she traveled through Iowa, Nebraska, and the Dakotas to observe the "Farmers Holiday" strike movement. Her report, "Feet in the Grass Roots," offers a brief history of the struggles of small farmers to keep ahead of bankruptcy and stresses their conviction that their protest was a modern version of the Boston Tea Party. She attended the Farmers Second National Conference in Chicago and afterwards wrote "Farmers Form a United Front," which analyzes the rise of militancy among farmers and outlines why they decided to demand a cancellation of their debts. After a summer visit to the Midwest, she wrote "The Farmer Looks Ahead," a vivid portrait of the effects of the drought of 1934 and the farmers' growing desperation.

Even as Herbst worked to establish herself as an intelligent commentator on social unrest and to bring to completion two of her most ambitious novels, *Pity Is Not Enough* and *The Executioner Waits*, on a personal level her life was in turmoil. While at the artists' colony Yaddo in the summer of 1932 she met Marion Greenwood, a young painter with whom she would remain involved until the following spring. When this relationship ended, Herbst and Herrmann, who had only recently begun to live apart after many months trying to behave as if the affair was having no effect on their emotional ties, attempted to resume their life together. But their marriage could not easily absorb discovery of her bisexuality and in 1934 they agreed on a separation that soon became definite.[11]

Early in 1935 Herbst went to Cuba to investigate revolutionary unrest for *New Masses*. From Havana she reported on the general strike that began in March of that year, then, eager to speak with the peasant rebels, made her way up the Oriente Mountains to the soviet Realengo 18, "where very few people, even Cubans, had gone to see the association they had formed to fight forcible eviction from the land they had tilled and lived on for many years."[12] When she returned from Cuba, she was given assignments by the *New York Post* and the *Nation* for a series of articles on the Nazi regime. In Germany she managed to gain the confidence of the underground opposition and was "with the first victims of Hitler's terror . . . when apparently it took a Socialist experience and imagination to guess the potential horror of what so many bourgeois German Jews could not."[13]

In March 1936 she received a Guggenheim Award in the field of the novel on the strength of the reputation she had built after the publication of the two volumes of her trilogy. She stayed the balance of the year in Erwinna, devoting herself completely to writing *Rope of Gold*. Breaking off work in December 1936, she went to Flint, Michigan, to observe the "sit-down strike" at General Motors, where workers were fighting for their right to collective bargaining. Early in 1937, she left for Spain to cover the Civil War for various periodicals.

While in Spain she stayed mainly in Madrid, with Hemingway, Dos Passos, and other correspondents at the Hotel Florida, and in little towns along the central front. The few articles she wrote speak intelligently and sympathetically about the International Brigades and about how Spanish peasants were reacting to the crisis. But as for "covering" the war, she would subsequently explain, she realized that there was no way she could "communicate the blind, spasmodic heaving of a society in agony—and *that* was the Civil War."[14] Besides, having witnessed the political in-fighting between the Communists, the Anarchists, and other groups, she had begun to suspect that the revolutionary movement was a great deal more complicated than she had thought. When the Loyalist side lost to Franco, Herbst's reaction was one of profound disappointment.

In the final years of the Depression decade the radical movement in America underwent an irrevocable process of disintegration. The ever-more-apparent totalitarianism of Soviet Russia, the rise of fascism, and the defeat of the Loyalists in Spain all helped dampen revolutionary fervor and hasten the decline of the social and political philosophies that had inspired many of the nation's writers. Although Herbst continued personally to maintain a leftist outlook, after 1937 active political radicalism was never again to be a central part of her life; and once she completed *Rope of Gold* in December 1938, like a number of her fellow authors she abandoned the writing of radical fiction.

For Modern Age publishers, she spent five months in South America in 1939, visiting Argentina, Brazil, Chile, Colombia, Cuba, and Uruguay to collect material for a book on United States–Latin American relations. Unprepared for an undertaking of this nature, she eventually discontinued the project. She returned to Erwinna where during 1940 and 1941 she wrote *Satan's Sergeants,* a novel about a Pennsylvania village. The poor critical reception of this book marked the beginning of the decline of her literary reputation.

After the bombing of Pearl Harbor Herbst volunteered her services to the Office of the Coordinator of Information in Washington where she worked at the German desk writing anti-Nazi propaganda for broadcast overseas. A few months later, she and an associate, Julia Older, were suddenly dismissed. Although the reasons for this action have never been made clear officially, Herbst claimed that in the fervor of the "Red Scare" she had been fired for having supported the Spanish Loyalists. Mrs. Older took immediate legal action and was offered reinstatement, but Herbst, outraged at being treated like a common criminal, chose not to file a complaint. Years after she would comment:

I had been fired abruptly, without being told the reasons and at a moment when I was due to be promoted to the New York office or overseas. Though this particular inquiry was to end with the approval of my qualifications by the investigators, they now began to look more like auditors who tally up the assets and liabilities of the alleged bankrupt before writing him off. I had the right of appeal, but I no longer wanted the post which now seemed to designate me more as a spook in a war poster than as an actor in a spectacular and moving pageant. What's more, I had no money to linger on in Washington and to petition, to hang around in corridors and "present my case." Nor was I convinced that the paper bullets our outfit was firing over the airways could have any effect.[15]

Following her experiences in Washington, Herbst returned to Erwinna for several months then went to Chicago where she stayed with a pleasant group of friends in the home of Dorothy Farrell, ex-wife of James T. Farrell, and kept busy by working for the Public Health Service, reviewing books for the *Chicago Sun Times*, and teaching writing in the radical Abraham Lincoln School.[16] Back in Erwinna in the fall of 1944, she began work on her last novel, *Somewhere the Tempest Fell* (1947). Reflecting her state of mind, this book deals with several characters' attempts to come to terms with the past.

Toward the end of the 1940s, Cold War concern about Communist infiltration crystallized around the case of Alger Hiss, a former State Department official who had been denounced as a spy by admitted former spy Whittaker Chambers. Since the case involved investigation of the Harold Ware Group, an underground Communist organization of which John Herrmann had been a part in the 1930s, Herbst was interviewed first by Hiss's lawyers and then by the FBI. Her testimony to the lawyers was suppressed because her substantiation of Chambers's claim that he had met Hiss as early as 1934 would have helped undermine the defense argument that Chambers was lying about everything. By the time Herbst met with the FBI agents, she was so fearful of further implicating Herrmann in the case that she gave out only vague information. Thus, her potentially important knowledge never became public.[17]

She was to have more dealings with the FBI during the McCarthy era of the 1950s when she was questioned at various times about her own activities in the 1930s and about those of other people.[18] In her interrogations she steadfastly maintained the point of view later expressed in her memoir "Yesterday's Road," that is, that the radical movement of the Depression decade had to be evaluated and judged in its proper historical context. These investigations ended in 1955 after she successfully challenged an attempt to deny her a passport.

Herbst's limited literary production in the 1950s, unlike her earlier writings, did not directly confront the complexities of contemporary society. Published in 1954, *New Green World* is a charming biographical study of the Pennsylvania naturalists John and William Bartram. Revealing a reverence for nature and a concern for conservation close to the Bartrams' own feelings, this book was praised for its insight and pleasant style. That same year, "Hunter of Doves," a story based on her friendship with Nathanael West, appeared in *Botteghe Oscure*, a well-respected Italian literary magazine. Intended as the first of "a series of stories about writers in our time and their predicament,"[19] it was the only part of the work that she ever finished.

Except for a relationship with the poet Jean Garrigue that began as a romantic attachment in the early 1950s and was later transformed into an enduring friendship, Herbst's life during the decade following World War II was generally quite lonely.[20] As the 1950s wore on, however, and all through the 1960s, she enjoyed frequent contact with many old and new friends, such as John Cheever, Edward Dahlberg, Alfred Kazin, Hilton Kramer, Saul Bellow, and Jane Mayhall. She also kept on writing. Living mainly in Erwinna, she devoted a large part of her time to work on her memoirs, which she wished to be both a personal history and a commentary on American writing since the 1920s. As her health declined, she completed only portions of this ambitious project. "The Starched Blue Sky of Spain," for which she received the Longview Award for Non-Fiction in 1961, re-creates her experiences during the Spanish Civil War; "A Year of Disgrace" deals with her life in New Preston and New York City in the late 1920s; "Yesterday's Road" speaks of her interrogation by civil service investigators at the time she was dismissed from her job in Washington. Her critical articles on Sherwood Anderson, Nathanael West, Edward Dahlberg, Ring Lardner, and Albert Rhys Williams provide further insight into her conception of the intellectual life of the 1920s and the 1930s.

After a long illness, Josephine Herbst died in a New York City hospital on January 28, 1969. In his memorial eulogy Alfred Kazin paid tribute to her vitality, forcefulness, and extraordinary humanity:

I have never known in my life any other writer who was so solid, so joyous, so giving, who was able to take difficulties so much in her stride, and who, even when she was getting pretty old and sick, made you see that flaming girl from Sioux City, and Berkeley and New York, Germany and Russia and Cuba and Spain, who was always getting mad about injustice and pompous stupidity, always radiating that marvelous sense of physical space and human possibilities that was the gift of the Middle West to so many writers of her generation.[21]

Chapter Two

A Note on
Narrative Technique

Even though Josephine Herbst wrote sparingly about her literary theories, from examination of scattered comments made during her career about the kinds of fiction she admired most and from insights into her vision of the writer's role in society provided in several critical essays published during the last two decades of her life, it is possible to derive an understanding of her ideas about both the creative process and the aims and functions of literature.

One of her most explicit statements about art and artists is expressed in an essay on Sherwood Anderson, in which she challenges those critics who wished Anderson had used his talents differently. Acknowledging that critics have the right to deplore writers' techniques, to quarrel with their judgments about society, and to set down responsible suggestions for future work, she also asks that they remember to allow them their aesthetic and ideological integrity. For writers, she maintains, cannot afford to question their own "essential nature" as they determine the range and direction of their work or to let themselves be coerced into distorting their individual responses to the historical and cultural circumstances in which they find themselves. To do so, she concludes, would be to betray one of the central aims of fiction:

The artist seeks to tell us what the world is or isn't; what it should be or even what it cannot be outside the realm of some transcendent dream. He doesn't start from a diagram but with a vision from nowhere, and he can afford to ignore his critics if they expect him to doubt his deepest impulses. He will have learned his craft, it is to be hoped, from the masters of literature, but what he himself says is likely to come from a compulsion to set down with unbearable accuracy what he conceives to be the truth.[1]

In other essays she explained how she thought writers might discover their particular "truths" and how they might learn to respond knowingly to their surroundings. Such discovery and such response, she felt, depended on their having a curious and questioning nature and on their willingness to explore their world fully, gathering the experiences and the impressions that might enable them to speak intelligently about it. Of herself in mid-career she observed:

The experience of life and the experience of writing are hard to separate. I know this country and that knowledge has back of [it] the perspective of living in other countries. I do not think it was chance that made me choose to go to four different colleges in widely separated geographical areas. It was the explorer's itch to know and to experience, which is a writer's way of learning through his own skin.[2]

Twenty years later she still felt that exploration was an important key to knowledge. "Roving," she wrote in 1956, "was good for the writer; to have been a reporter undoubtedly informed Ring Lardner, Ernest Hemingway, Stephen Crane. To know far more than he may ever use is imperative for the writer."[3]

Herbst also believed that in order to understand better their social and cultural milieu writers needed to adopt an attitude of detachment from it. As she put it, the artist's task is one of reconciling "fanaticism"—that is, willed exposure to experience and direct confrontation of crucial problems—with "serenity." "Taken alone each is dangerous, yet except through integration of the two there is no art. For nothing can be accomplished without fanaticism and without serenity nothing can be perceived in its own identity."[4] Only the inner balance achieved by this commingling of experience and contemplation would, in her view, prepare writers to comment acutely and lucidly on complex contemporary issues.

Because she respected each writer's personal vision, she did not presume to describe how social observation and critique should take shape in fiction. But she did assert that she could not think of "any really important imaginative writing in this country or any other, whether it be Gogol's *Dead Souls* or Flaubert's *Madame Bovary,* or the novels of Thomas Hardy, which isn't basically critical of the social order."[5] For this reason she was deeply disturbed in the early 1950s by what she termed some young writers' "genteel retreat from a period too complicated to confront easily." What was lost in this retreat, she felt, was precisely that sense of the encircling world that she valued so highly:

What seems to be missing in a good deal of contemporary writing is a sense of the world. The world around us. For some time now we have had so many writers trailing their own nervous systems, premonitions, fantasies and horrors, that perhaps the time has come to dig up man, the guilty worm, and see him in relation to an actual world. It has gone so far that the word "actual" may start an argument. I mean it, just the same, in its Jane Austen sense, its Flaubertian sense, its Tolstoian sense. To insist on this point of the actual is, practically speaking, avant garde.[6]

She interpreted this lack of a felt sense of external reality as the consequence of a deliberate refusal to explore and ponder social and political phenomena, an attitude, she feared, that eventually would estrange young writers from life altogether, robbing them of insight and rendering their creative powers sterile. She explained that she was not merely encouraging the young writers whom she did not name (and whom she may have misinterpreted) to return to the tradition of social realism, but was rather reiterating her firm conviction that "there is no such thing as a writer untouched by his time." To support this claim she cited such authors as Kafka and Dostoevski who, although they dealt with regions beyond usual human experience and employed many "unrealistic" techniques, nonetheless created striking metaphors for the general human condition and offered penetrating observations on their sociopolitical environment.

Bearing witness to Herbst's artistic views are those consistent elements in her novels that constitute her characteristic thematic concerns and mode of expression. In keeping with her belief that writers' most fertile sources of subject matter are their personal experiences and the insights they obtain through direct confrontation with their social and cultural environment, in all of her novels she draws on scenes, persons, and events from her own experience. She uses this material, submerged in the characters and events of her fiction, to conduct a careful and continuous examination of life in America and of the nature of human experience in general. Her concern is not with the facts of her own experience but with interpretation of these facts, not with a simple documentation of events but with discovery of their larger meanings. Of her decision to base her trilogy on what she had learned "through the skin" of her ancestors, for instance, she observed:

It seemed to me that such a family could be a test tube to show the general workings of something beyond the significance of mere family history. I wanted not only family relations, births, deaths, marriages, and personal problems but the relation of people to society as well as the relation of people to one another. . . . I have been excited to show that the fascinating interest is the mixture of lives rather than the inner brooding of one life.[7]

Her narrative techniques and literary structures appear to have grown naturally out of her philosophy of subject matter. She apparently decided early in her career that the kind of perspective provided by a concealed narrator would best serve her purposes in making the matter of her life illuminate general human and social issues. The device of the concealed narrator gave her access to the lives and minds of all her characters without limiting her to the point of view of any one of them. She could therefore shift perspective frequently to present their subjective reactions and at the same time maintain an objective distance from each of them. Her characteristic narrator, though close to the people in her novels, is neither wholly identifiable with them nor, though aware of the overall pattern of their experiences, so authoritative as an omniscient narrator might be. For these reasons, this narrator does not impose arbitrary order or meaning on the material presented but instead acts as the medium through which real events and felt experiences reach the reader. In other words, the Herbst narrator functions as a surrogate for her "ideal writer," that sensitive person who roves, observes, discerns, and points out relationships, and, without offering any overt interpretations, directs the reader toward a recognition of the general implications of the experiences and events presented.

Impulses similar to those that led Herbst to favor a concealed narrator influenced the way in which she chose to structure her books. She wanted to deal with a variety of social and cultural dilemmas and to reveal but not to appear to impose definitions on the complexities of human behavior and experience, complexities for which she felt no easy solutions could be posed but which an author should nonetheless strive to present compassionately. Thus, in none of her novels is she interested in fashioning a well-made plot; instead, she simultaneously develops a number of equally important narrative strands which she weaves together to create an overall narrative pattern that communicates meaning not through explicit detail but with illuminating suggestiveness.

The kind of structure she always employed permits relatively little space for developing individual characters. In novels without a dominant story line, such as those by John Dos Passos or Sherwood Anderson, characters tend to become part of a total pattern. Herbst refused to concentrate her central meanings in any protagonist, choosing instead to embody in each character a different aspect of the social or human condition under examination. But although she never explored the depth and breadth of any single character, she managed to make many of them believable as individuals, through a method of portraiture that lies somewhere between the conventions of the psychological novel and those of sociological fiction. She conceived of her characters not only as psychic entities but as social and political beings, not only as products and victims of their environment but as people who want to transcend the limited and limiting circumstances of their lives. In presenting them, she thus gave equal importance to expression of their inner experiences and to delineation of their relationships to their surroundings. In this way, without becoming excessively stereotyped, the individual characters also convey the characteristic social dilemmas of their worlds.

In none of her novels is the language especially rich in implication, for Herbst was apparently not accustomed or inclined to convey her observations in symbolic terms or metaphoric language. But though simple, her almost colloquial style is nonetheless suggestive. At times her writing approaches "stream of consciousness" although, just as her choice of perspective and structure foster a certain dramatic distance, so too her handling of language does not permit complete immersion in her characters' lives. When they speak and when they think, the words they use are evidently their words, cast into narrative form and conveyed from a third-person point of view. However, through shifts in tone and style, the author alternately projects her readers into the minds of her protagonists and pulls them back to survey the scene from a broader vantage point, thus making them as she herself wished to be, "participants" and "observers."

In terms of general subject matter and of overall stylistic and technical approach, Herbst's novels reflect significant trends of the three decades in which they were written. Her books from the 1920s, *Nothing Is Sacred* and *Money for Love,* offer a critique of the middle class and are written in the concise, economic manner generally associated with Ernest Hemingway. In the trilogy, *Pity Is Not Enough, The Executioner Waits,* and *Rope of Gold,* written in the 1930s, she uses techniques of the panoramic social realism typical of much fiction of that decade and employs a style of dialogue that faithfully reproduces the sounds of living conversation. Her later novels, *Satan's Sergeants* and *Somewhere the Tempest Fell*, share with the work of other writers of the 1940s an emphasis on moral problems and on crises of personal identity.

How successfully Herbst accomplished the artistic goals she set herself in writing each of these novels and what insights the novels offer into the nature of American life are the main topics of the next three chapters.

Chapter Three
Early Novels

In "Iowa Takes to Literature," an article published in the *American Mercury* in 1926,[1] Josephine Herbst's description of small-town women's literary clubs reveals attitudes similar to those of satirists of the middle class like H. L. Mencken and Sinclair Lewis, writers who in protest against the directions American society was taking in the post-World War I period conducted an assault on the manners and mores of the bourgeoisie. The linguistic and formal experimentations of other writers in the 1920s, she reports in her memoir "A Year of Disgrace,"[2] frequently evoked her keen enthusiasm, for she understood the importance and the necessity of their efforts to forge appropriate strategies for coping with modern experience. When she came to write her novels *Nothing Is Sacred* (1928) and *Money for Love* (1929), however, she avoided biting satire, preferring to investigate the social dimension of the middle class in a straightforward manner. Similarly, from the myriad of new modes of literary expression made available to writers in the 1920s who wished to explore the strain and crisis of the times, she selected and made her own not one of the more daringly innovative but a modernized version of realism.

Serious commentary on social conditions and conventions and a method of writing that blended some aspects of realism with such modernist devices as authorial detachment from the material of the story, use of multiple narratives, and portrayal of the inner consciousness of the individual would be traits typical of all her fiction. During the 1920s she used this approach and these techniques to study the effects of the collapse of traditional values and behavior patterns on ordinary American citizens. In *Nothing Is Sacred,* by means of an art that admits of no sentimentalizing, she set herself the task of evoking the uncertainties, the frustrations, the loneliness, and the pain average people were experiencing as they tried to adapt to a world they did not completely understand. In *Money for Love* she focused on a group of people trapped by their lack of purpose and loss of sense of personal identity.

Nothing Is Sacred

Nothing Is Sacred (1928) is constructed on five relatively independent story lines, each related to a single character and composed of a series of episodes that gradually reveal the nature of that character's private dilemma. Episodes referring to one or another of these narratives follow continuously in the text, with only an occasional double spacing to indicate a pause or shift of scene. None of the characters assumes the role of major protagonist, whose centrality would serve to organize and focus the book's concerns; instead, all seem to be "lesser" figures in whose experiences are located partial insights into the book's themes and issues. The novel also offers a variety of points of view, for it is told in the voice of a concealed narrator who continually shifts perspective to report on the subjective experiences of whichever character is in the spotlight. This narrator generally stays within the confines of each character's awareness and rarely makes observations beyond those appropriate to his or her individual psychology.

The action of the novel covers several months in the life of a middle-class Midwestern family. The first few scenes, which set the tense emotional atmosphere in which these people will be seen throughout the entire story, show the family mobilizing to avoid the social disgrace that would inevitably follow if it were to become widely known that one of them, Harry Norland, has been embezzling money from his lodge treasury to cover the debts he has accumulated to maintain himself in a manner beyond what his salesman's salary permits. When Harry announces his delinquency there is already hostility between him and the rest of the family, since they have always disapproved of his spendthrift ways and condescending attitude toward them. Nevertheless, once they realize that his lodge brothers intend to make a moral example of him, they agree to help out in order to spare the family's good name. Mrs. Winter, Harry's mother-in-law, puts another mortgage on the house she has been trying for years to pay off; the rest of his relatives contribute what money they can and promise vigilance over his behavior in the future. Efforts to overcome the consequences of Harry's theft, however, occupy only a small part of the remaining narrative, the bulk of which focuses on the private lives of individual family members, each of whom, feeling thwarted by external circumstances, has been questing unsuccessfully for fulfillment.

The author makes it clear that all of her characters are motivated by a legitimate desire for happiness and seek, in particular, love and a sense of personal worth. For their repeated failures to find what they most desire, her novel suggests two reasons. The first of these evolves from an implied vision of human beings as blundering creatures whose principal defect is a tendency to profit only marginally from experience. With the exception of Mrs. Winter, these characters approach life with ideas that have no basis in fact, are hopelessly self-absorbed, and have no taste for seeing things in their proper perspective. Accordingly, not only do they fail to find fulfillment but, lacking the realistic and self-critical attitudes that make knowledge possible, they learn nothing from their blunders. The other cause for the haplessness of their quests relates to the nature of American society in the 1920s, which in this novel is depicted in a state of dislocation. Each of the characters represents one aspect of Herbst's vision of this causality within the novel.

Harry's devil-may-care quest for material goods, though admittedly carried to an extreme, reflects the role middle-class Americans were asked to play in the 1920s, when economic frugality seemed antithetical to industrial expansion and people were encouraged to spend their money to increase their comfort, prove their mettle, and enjoy "the good life." A materialist who in accordance with current middle-class thinking equates financial success with personal merit, Harry is ashamed because he is not well off; he devotes his energies to stealing what life seems to have capriciously withheld from him, never worrying about the inevitable results of his behavior:

Where he was going eventually, Harry never considered. He played the game childishly not knowing how he was ever to pay up the total indebtedness which now amounted to more than three thousand dollars. Besides his account with the lodge he owed money all over town, yet he went ahead, buying new furniture, buying a grand piano, buying a car, paying a little on each, as he knew very well a good many other men were doing, all living from day to day with an air of prosperity.[3]

In addition to being hypnotized by his consumer-oriented culture, Harry lives without exercising his reflective intellect, without ideas of his own, and without emotions. Even after the scandal, his devotion to the values of materialism and his lack of personal dignity persist, and he feels no remorse for his delinquency or compassion for his relatives who besides being publicly humiliated have been forced to assume the burden of his debts. His major worry is simply that from now on he will have to live without feeling "important."

The parts of the narrative devoted to Harry's wife Julia and her two sisters catch the undercurrent of some of the transformations taking place in women's lives in the 1920s. Discontent with her status as wife and mother creates in Julia Norland an emotional void which she tries to fill by engaging in a series of extramarital affairs; her plight is complicated by the fact that she thoroughly succumbs to the image of the sexy woman as the standard of attractiveness which was even then being promoted in the mass media. Indeed, the primary motivation behind her experiments with adultery is her desire for an emotional involvement that measures up to those presented in popular novels and ladies magazines, her major resource for information about life. "She read these stories and wondered why nothing like that ever happened to her. In spite of all she had discovered for herself about men she was still anxious to discover more. She half believed and disbelieved that women ever felt the way the stories made out" (146–47).

Her romantic hopes, like her husband's illusions about the efficacy of money as an elevating force, are commented on ironically by the crude realities of her life and are shown to have distorted her perception of reality. In fact, she tries to convince herself that encounters with her suitors are worth risking her middle-class respectability, even though these men are so clumsy and unimaginative that they totally contradict all the mass-media images of the ideal lover. Nor is her behavior seriously affected by her husband's economic difficulties or by her duties to her children or her ailing mother. Instead, in a pathetically comic way, her dream world topples only when she learns that she must have her teeth removed, a devastating change that threatens to destroy her attractiveness and to leave her with the prospect of an empty and meaningless future. Insincerity, irresponsibility, and triviality thus characterize her conduct both during her efforts to find excitement and satisfaction in sex and after external circumstances have forced her to give up her search.

Julia's flaunting of traditional morality and her desire to partake of the "glamorous" side of life in the 1920s are repeated in a minor key in the story of her self-centered elder sister, Hazel Bell, who is likewise captivated by a new image of woman, the young and carefree flapper whose life style she tries briefly but desperately to imitate. Married to a hardworking but dull man, embittered at not having had children, and with nothing to occupy or amuse her and nothing to look forward to, Hazel at first takes refuge in picturing herself as a victim of cruel circumstances. At a certain point, however, drama-tization of her misfortunes is no longer sufficient and she feels that she must act. Too timid to consent to infidelity, she tries to find an antidote to her problems by bobbing her hair and going to local night spots with her nephew Ted, pretending to herself that "people who saw them together thought of them as a young couple" (45). When Ted wearies of her company, Hazel merely returns with increased ir-ritation and depression to the petty routines of her daily existence, without ever having realized that the strongest force oppressing her is her own self-deception, that she is in fact sexually repressed and terrified at the thought of growing old in a society that exalts youth.

An inside view of the zestful, fun-loving culture which so attracts Julia and Hazel is offered in the episodes that describe their younger sister Hilda who, unable to stand the stultifying atmosphere of her small town and unwilling to repeat her sisters' frustrating experi-ences, moves to Chicago where she trusts that in the exciting and varied environment of a big city she can find an authentic and grat-ifying life. With bright hopes for the future she marries Ross, a handsome and free-thinking young man. However, she soon discovers that while she agrees with her husband's refusal to worship money, she does not like their tight economic situation, and that al-though she too professes to accept the moral codes of the rising generation, she is terrified when she learns that he has been unfaith-ful. Caught between a deep-rooted adherence to the bourgeois values that she wishes to overcome and a sense of uneasiness with the new modes of behavior that she tries to adopt, she is at first simply diso-riented. Later, convinced that while she can change the outward form of her life she can never assure herself of inner peace, she ends up by abandoning all her hopes and accepting her situation.

The only character whose interior life remains relatively intact in the sisters' crumbling world is their mother Mrs. Winter, whose sim-ple faith in the primacy of the family, the importance of sacrifice, and the necessity for patient loving enables her to meet life courageously, an achievement which the younger people, for whom "nothing is sa-cred," cannot match. And yet she too must come to terms with feel-ings of frustration. She had trusted that marriage would enrich her daughters' lives but is forced to acknowledge that it has deepened their discontent. Because she knows they consider her principles out-moded, she must refrain from counseling them and watch helplessly while they flounder. Finally, just as she is beginning to look forward to a tranquil old age, she is obliged to resign herself to an imminent death by cancer. Her quiet dignity in responding to loss of her position as a role model for her daughters and to the sad knowledge that her life is slipping away, as well as her refusal to allow these experiences to alienate her completely from the people she loves, render her the most powerful and appealing figure in this novel. Herbst has set the old-fashioned values by which she lives in revealing contrast to the nervous groping of her children.

The presentations of the other characters are not wholly unsympathetic but are rather designed to invite the reader's understanding of the motivations and personal shortcomings that deform their lives. By maintaining a careful balance between exposing the public and private causes of their failures, Herbst portrays them as individuals defeated both by a cultural conditioning that evokes in them dreams that are destined never to be fulfilled, and by a lack of the intellectual and spiritual vitality that might have enabled them to use their negative experiences as points from which to revise radically their outlook and behavior.

A Somber Study of Middle-Class Americans

Although no contemporary reviewer gave evidence of having fully discerned the underlying social and moral significance of *Nothing Is Sacred,* critical opinions about the meaning of the novel and about its artistry provide suggestions for further analysis. Some reviewers criticized both Herbst's choice of subject matter and her craftsmanship, laying against her the charge that facticity had smothered her imagination. Their point of view was summarized by Clifton Fadiman, who said in the *Nation* that her novel offered "the life of a mean, gray, middle-class American family, set down in a mean, gray, middle-class American prose. . . . Fiercely honest as this type of writing is, it leads one to suspect its intrinsic importance."[4] Ford Madox Ford, however, expressing his belief that the modern novelist must avoid focusing on the heroic and the unusual and instead attempt to illuminate the actual world, called the book "a distinguished first novel" precisely for the skill with which the author engaged the reader in her "quite commonplace" characters and events. He asserted that it proved

There is no reason why the story of a small-town family should not be as interesting as any detective-romance—the trouble usually is that [unlike Herbst] the narrators of such tales begin with the thesis that the life de-

scribed has by them been found uninteresting and that they must therefore
make an uninteresting story out of it.[5]

In truth, the substance of the narrative in this book is neither as en-
grossing as Ford insists nor as simplistic as Fadiman believes. Somber
and not wholly accessible on a first reading, it involves both exploration of the dreary lives and bitter disappointments of a specific
group of lower middle-class Americans and creation of the general
impressions that modern experience is inevitably frustrating and that
individuals are forever imprisoned in their own limitations.

Critics taking up the question of literary influences noted connections between *Nothing Is Sacred* and works by some of Herbst's contemporaries. The commentator for the *New York Times* mentioned
that "the simplicity of her idiom, the economy of her method and
the unemotionalized detachment of her point of view" resembled
characteristics of the early writings of Ernest Hemingway, but did
not feel obliged to label her an imitator because "she makes us feel
that the plain, compact, sometimes drab style she has adopted is the
only possible style for the story she has undertaken."[6] Introducing her
to readers of the *New Republic* as "the latest addition to the Anderson-
Lardner-Hemingway school of fiction," T. S. Matthews remarked
"she is most welcome. There will never be many successful pupils in
this class, for the balance between dullness and starkness will never
become any easier to find."[7] Finally, Katherine Anne Porter, besides
agreeing that the energy of the novel came not from its subject matter but from the author's treatment of it, felt the book possessed so-
lider qualities of characterization and style than many more pretentious
works. The protagonists, she observed, "are human beings, born in
a certain set of circumstances to a certain mode of existence, but the
individual creature clearly shows through the pattern behavior of the
group." And of the style she wrote:

the sentences are short, the words are simple, and still the prose has poetic
grace and style. It is not angular, spare, stark, dry, or any of the more
kindly synonyms for jerky dullness. It is beautiful and full with the fullness
of a perfect economy and final choice of phrase. It is all in one piece from
beginning to end, and must be read line by line, or you will miss something
important to the story.[8]

All of these favorable comments are too broadly stated to capture the
essence of Herbst's mode of narration in *Nothing Is Sacred,* which, in

addition to being less beautiful than suggested in Porter's description, is more peculiar to Herbst than critics implied. For while it is true that her prose resembles plain, everyday American conversation and that her narrative strategies are simple and economic, she, like the writers cited by critics as her mentors, used these linguistic and technical devices in a manner appropriate to the specific aims of her novel.

Herbst's narrative method in *Nothing Is Sacred* is typified in the section describing the evening when Hazel tells Julia about Harry's embezzling. Running for twenty-five pages, this section consists of five scenes of equal length, each centering on one or two characters. In the first, Hazel complains to her husband Ralph that making her break the news to Julia is merely the most recent of her family's many "impositions" on her: " 'You might know I'd be the one that would have to tell Julia. When there's anything unpleasant to do we are always the ones to do it' " (41). Her bitter tone leads Ralph to wearily review their life together, memories which indicate that she has never been able to put into effect any of her plans to change her life. As his recollections reach the present time, the focus shifts to Hazel to disclose her fantasizing about her friendship with her nephew Ted, a relationship which will be shown to be another dead-end solution to her problems.

The next scene opens with a brief dialogue between Mrs. Winter and Hazel, who has stopped at her parents' home before going to see Julia. " 'Well, here I go,' said Hazel, 'I'd rather be shot.'. . . She rose and Ralph, who had been standing silently, his closeness expressing his sympathy, followed her out of the house" (48–49). After she leaves, her mother recalls her own opposition to Julia's marriage because she was sure Julia was not in love with Harry and how "when she learned Julia was going around discreetly with other men . . . she began to take Harry's part, and to wonder if perhaps he might have been different if Julia had been wiser at the beginning of her married life" (50). Then Mrs. Winter remembers an early romance of her own and, glancing over at Hilda, speculates hopefully about whether she and her husband Ross are sharing that same exhilaration.

The focus of the following scene is on Hilda. Ironically, she is evaluating her motives for suspecting Ross is having an affair and is thinking back on the early days of their relationship. Her thoughts concisely communicate both her tense emotional state and the qualities of mind, especially fearfulness and sentimentality, that have brought her to her present impasse:

Today another letter from Ross had come, she knew she should trust him, be satisfied, but she wasn't. She had read and reread the one page letter, drummed off hastily on his typewriter. "Dearest" it began, and ended "with love." Between the beginning and the end there was nothing about her. . . . She compared this letter with all the letters she had gotten from him since she had come home to visit her mother. She looked them all over, critically, one by one, and then she got out the little bundle of his first letters that he had written her over a year ago when they first became lovers. . . . When she had gotten these letters she had not valued them as she did now. The time had to pass when he was able to write in that way to her. Now she was really beginning to wonder what she might have done to keep him that way always. (52–53)

The scene ends with Hilda and her mother separately wondering what Hazel and Julia are saying to each other.

The sisters' conversation is taken up in the next episode, which after stressing Hazel's nervousness and Julia's anger, shows these emotions subsiding as Hazel reassures her sister that the family will help out and as Julia admits that such a crisis was inevitable. The section ends with Julia and Harry having an argument, then going to bed where each is absorbed in silent recriminations against the other.

These five scenes successively develop specific problems of specific characters and are linked together both on the level of plot, by the element of Harry's theft, and thematically, through revelation of the characters' common failings and their underlying if sometimes tense emotional attachments to one another. No details extraneous to these matters are introduced. The scenes are narrated in an intentionally flat style that contributes both to underscoring the drab nature of the world and the people it depicts and to conveying the desired central effect—one of social, moral, and psychological limitation.

In the novel as a whole Herbst employs the same dominant techniques. Every element of her narrative points to a narrow and degrading sphere of possibilities. There is a paucity of the sensuous detail that usually gives fiction substance and density; instead, Herbst relies on summary descriptions of small, uninteresting interior settings and of characters who are never made to come into sharp focus through revealing adjectives or imagery but are simply associated with a few concrete items, such as Harry's imported cigars, Julia's cold cream, and Hazel's bag of chocolate drops, palpable emblems that stand out in stark juxtaposition to the spareness of the rest of the description and that effectively comment on the gap between the characters' aspirations and the commonplace nature of their actual condition.

In the meditations and brief dialogues which make up the bulk of the narrative, the author uses ordinary words, generally simple declarative sentences, and incorrect grammar and slang whenever suitable to the character thinking or speaking. The aim of this language, however, is not precisely to reproduce American speech authentically but rather to create a stylized version of it, keyed like everything else in the book to a deliberately controlled minimum. To this end the author strips the spoken idiom of most of its charm and personality through rigid economy of wording, sharp reduction of adjectives and imaginative phrasing, and avoidance of rhythmic variety. In the process she fashions a language reflective of the narrow fictional world it describes.

Money for Love

The private dramas in *Money for Love* (1929) are in a sense continuations of those presented in *Nothing Is Sacred,* for if the characters in that book are captured in the process of being disillusioned by life, these people are shown acting out the consequences of such disillusionment. This novel, however, lacks the suggestive sociological import of the first because the author limits the scope of her investigation to matters that relate to her characters' emotional lives, without attempting to illuminate the underlying structures of the contemporary world.

At the center of this novel, which is set in New York, is Harriet Everist, a modestly talented actress who interrupted her career and fled home to the Midwest after her married lover, the playwright Bruce Jones, had forced her to have an abortion. Several years have passed when the story opens and Harriet is back in New York and in love with Joseph Roberts, a widower and former medical student. She is also jobless and in need of money. Knowing that Bruce has become immensely successful in his career and having always felt that he owes her some kind of settlement for the past, she decides to tell him about her economic difficulties. After eliciting from him a vague promise to help out, she rushes to tell Joseph that Bruce wants to give her five thousand dollars. With this money, she explains, they can marry and go to Vienna where he can start studying medicine again.

Reality, however, is more complicated than Harriet admits. Two serious obstacles stand between her and her goals. Bruce has no intention of giving her such a large sum of money, whether out of conscience or out of sentiment, while Joseph, who has little ambition of any kind, is less interested in studying medicine than she pretends and is also very hesitant about getting permanently involved with her, especially over a question of money. Their relationship is further obstructed by his sister-in-law Louise, who keeps urging him to be loyal to his wife's memory. Despite these difficulties, Harriet does not lose heart. After Bruce sends her a few dollars, barely the amount anyone would offer a needy acquaintance, she resolves to "get tough" and threatens to send his wife the love letters he wrote to her. Bruce tells her that the letters are worthless but after realizing how desperate she is, he begins to bargain and eventually sends her a check for one thousand dollars, two hundred more than her last hysterical request. While negotiating with Bruce, she schemes to take advantage of Joseph's easygoing nature, and through constant beseeching finally breaks down his defenses. The novel ends with a wedding, a party, and a ride to the piers because the newlyweds are going to Vienna, just as Harriet had planned.

Irony of situation permeates Harriet's story. Bruce's wife knew of their affair, so blackmail was never a real possibility; the money he finally supplied was given out of pity rather than fear. Harriet need not have been so dishonest and manipulative toward the weak-willed Joseph, whom she probably could have managed to marry without offering him money; moreover, since her ties to him are so tenuous, her maneuvering has merely set the stage for further irritation and disappointment for both of them.

Throughout the novel Herbst plays these ironies against her own ruthless fidelity in delineating Harriet's spiritual bankruptcy. In consequence, the reader's attitude toward her protagonist oscillates between condemnation of her petty scheming and pity for the fact that she has such an inadequate self-image that she treats herself as a piece of merchandise. Herbst quite frankly reveals Harriet to be a common and not very clever woman who belittles her relationship with Joseph by considering it primarily as a practical arrangement and who degrades herself in her tawdry dealings with Bruce. Yet she also invites understanding of the events and personal deficiencies that make Harriet behave as she does. She stresses that it was the painful dissolution of Harriet's earlier affair that destroyed her confidence and brought her to the conviction that to achieve at least a modest amount of happiness in the future she had to put restraints on her true feelings and behave toward others in a calculating way.

The narrative lines relating to the other main characters, Joseph and Louise, are explorations essentially of the same dissatisfaction with life and inability to cope with guilt and loss that impel Harriet to suppress any meaningful emotional life she might have had and to resign herself to operating unhappily within very limited horizons. After the death of his first wife as a result of an abortion he did not want her to have, Joseph stagnates for three years. He becomes involved in marriage with Harriet not out of love or over money but because by that time he has lost even his capacity to be aimless in his own way. Louise's conviction that she must spend her life revering her sister's memory because she did nothing to prevent her from having her abortion causes her to give up the idea of becoming a scientist, to take the most depressing jobs she can find, and to regard anyone who makes friendly overtures as an interloper.

Along with reducing the range of her observation in this novel, Herbst also compresses the various elements of her form. She sharply circumscribes the time span of the story, which occupies only the few weeks between Harriet's first contact with Bruce and her marriage to Joseph; she limits it spatially almost exclusively to Harriet's tiny apartment; and she articulates the main action, Harriet's attempt at double-edged blackmail, in very few incidents presented with a minimum of suspense and surprise and no emotional peaks or minor climaxes. Her characterizations are similarly curtailed. Though the external circumstances of her characters' lives change during the course of the story, at the end, because the characters have never experienced a moment of illumination, they are in the same psychological condition in which they were first introduced, defeated by earlier tragedies and lacking insight and strong inner goals. Finally, to bring her language in line with the shape of the rest of her narrative, Herbst employs an even more flat and commonplace style than in *Nothing Is Sacred.*

A Dubious Accomplishment

For varying reasons, reviewers uniformly expressed dissatisfaction with *Money for Love.* Katherine Anne Porter, for instance, disturbed by the bitterness that Herbst displayed toward her material, reversed the praise she had given the previous book:

In her second novel, Josephine Herbst strips her vocabulary to fighting trim and goes for poor lost middle western human nature with a kind of cold detached ferocity that makes my hair rise. . . . These people . . . are fascinating in a fearful way, because a good artist, perfectly in command of her method, has for her own mysterious reasons chosen to assemble them: her lack of human pity is her own business. She has made a fine job of destruction. What, precisely, is she trying to kill?[9]

Other commentators took exception to the characterizations and the style, complaining that "the heroine . . . remains to the very end a two-dimensional creation"[10] and the language "is kept on a dead level of drab phrases, free of exaltation or elevation of any sort whatever."[11] And in the course of an article for the *Nation* about contemporary literature Isidor Schneider described Herbst as one of those writers who in slavish imitation of some of Hemingway's techniques were making a "fetish of simplicity" by attempting "to suppress literary personality or 'style,' to substitute actual colloquial speech for conventional literary conversation, and to rule out all effects designed to stimulate emotion." Revealing that he knew Herbst personally, he further lamented that she did not utilize in her fiction the same "genuine and abundant" narrative powers she exhibited in conversation.[12]

In a reply in the *Nation* Herbst expressed dismay at Schneider's description of "the Hemingway school," pointing out that many writers from different periods have endeavored "to write in the language of the day rather than in the high literary tongue in vogue at the time." But she also admitted she had written *Money for Love* in an effort to see how far she could stretch the sparse method of characterization and unadorned language she had employed in her first novel, and that she herself was not pleased with the results of her experiment:

I wrote [*Money for Love*] deliberately with the intent of discovering just how far a rigid acceptance of a certain method would take me. I never liked the book, do not like it now, and have always considered it pinched. But the people were pared to the bone, not to be realistic or natural, as you claim, but to suggest an even completer bareness of life than the actuality of the characters could portray. I believe you assume too much when you conclude that the end and aim of *my* writing, at least, is to be natural. Frankly, I think it is quite unimportant, to be natural or not to be, to use colloquialisms or not to use them, so long as you attain what you set out to attain. In "Money For Love" . . . I meant to get an overtone that would be more convincing than "reality." I succeeded so well that I never want to do this sort of thing again. But in adhering to this method I was under no compulsion to exalt "simplicity" but to attain a certain end. The machinery dominated the content in this case, and not by chance. I believe such a procedure always fails.[13]

Schneider and the other critics were justified in their overall negative reactions to *Money for Love,* even if some of them would appear to have attacked the book for reasons secondary to its main failing. For Herbst *was* successful in handling her tight narrow form. Unfortunately, by choosing to limit herself to exploring such a small corner of existence and to focusing on characters so uniformly lacking in spirit, she expended her talents on what was probably an insignificant undertaking.

Her next books, the trilogy, are in terms of scope and social observation the complete opposite to *Money for Love.* Yet as she broke through to larger content and more complex form, Herbst did not slight what she had gained through her literary experiences in the 1920s. Her technical experiments gave her skill in working with a series of interrelated dramas that would aid her considerably in writing her trilogy, while her development of a language that approximated the spoken idiom would help her give added fidelity to her representations of average Americans. Finally, some of the insights into human nature these books contained would be incorporated into the broader vision of life she would express in her next major work of fiction.

Chapter Four
The Trilogy

During the 1930s, like many other intellectuals concerned about the grave social and economic problems in America, Josephine Herbst turned to Marxism. In this philosophy she found what seemed to her not only a plausible explanation of how America had reached its crisis, but also a coherent proposal for the resolution of its present chaos and preparation for a more stable future. Hers was neither a sudden conversion nor a fashionable allegiance to radical ideas. As early as 1927, after the execution of Sacco and Vanzetti, she had begun to redefine her conception of the intellectual's relationship to the larger society, a process that in a few years took her "as far left as you can go."[1] Her political journalism throughout the Depression decade, based as it was on contact with the protagonists of crucial uprisings at home and abroad, attests to the depth of her convictions and to her acceptance of rebellion as a justifiable reaction to decades of repression. However, she was reluctant to align herself with any official revolutionary movement and never acted as a spokesperson for any group.

For Josephine Herbst, radicalism meant formulating ideas about the nature of the problems facing America and about ways of solving them, and then testing these ideas in her own life and art. She agreed with those who felt that capitalism had reached a watershed and that American society was disintegrating so rapidly that the nation would achieve stability again only through a drastic revision of its social and economic philosophy. She was therefore impatient with the programs of the New Deal, which she considered to be attempts to reform capitalism rather than instruments for full-scale social change. She also shared the belief, current among radical intellectuals, that history was heading toward some kind of final conflict. Dissatisfaction with age-old inequalities seemed to be reaching the breaking point, and when the tension exploded, she felt, it would herald a new era characterized by socialist values, in contradistinction to the individualistic urges that had supported capitalism. Finally, she grew convinced that no intellectual could afford to stand aloof from what was happening in

America. Writers in particular now seemed to have before them significant responsibilities. They needed to confront artistically the complex problems of the decade and to set forth structural alternatives to the existing order. For, as Herbst later remarked, "in a period of demoralization and terror it was no bad thing to try to act, however mistakenly or inadequately, as the conscience of the age."[2]

Her major literary undertaking during this period was to be nothing less than a reinterpretation of America's social and economic institutions from the time of the Civil War through the Depression. In this work she intended to expose the tragic reality of American life, a reality she conceived of as an ongoing and often bitter struggle between proponents of two distinct American "dreams," the promise of equality for all and the right of the individual to strive for and protect personal success. This reality would be presented from the standpoint of those whom it had injured most, those whose human potential had been wasted because they believed that capitalism encompassed both dreams, worked hard to achieve them, and then failed. It would show how this drama repeated itself for generations before the Depression gave rise to the diffusion of radical sentiments and before the working class began to question the validity of the system itself. In essence, the author hoped to explain why capitalism had for so long been able to distort the ideals of the American people, how it had brought the country to its current state of confusion, and how various forces were gathering to overthrow it.

A ready-made body of subject matter was at hand to be drawn on for this ambitious undertaking. Herbst carried in her intellectual baggage an extensive laboratory record of American history, based on information about her own family, which had participated in many of the great adventures of the American people since pre-Revolutionary days. As she recalled:

I was brought up on my mother's nostalgia for the East and her admiration for those members of her family who had ventured, often to their downfall, dramatized for me my entire conception of American life. . . . The family for generations had kept diaries and letters and the first inkling I had of the complexity and significance of people in relation to one another and the world came from those documents. Living seemed constantly fertilized by the tragic burden each generation passed on to the next.[3]

She would of course need to turn her family's history into fiction and to fill in the background necessary for communicating the flavor of the eras through which these people had lived. Most of all, she would need to interpret their "tragic burden," so that their story could serve as a convincing argument against capitalism and also convey a deeply felt human significance. These were some of the tasks facing her as she began work on what, over the course of eight years, would become the Trexler-Wendel trilogy: *Pity Is Not Enough* (1933), *The Executioner Waits* (1934), and *Rope of Gold* (1939).

In seeking a form suitable for transforming her family history into fiction, Josephine Herbst drew inspiration from literary collectivism, a method of narration not dissimilar to that which she had employed in her early novels. It is a technique like that used by John Dos Passos in *Manhattan Transfer* and the trilogy *U. S. A.* In contrast to the traditional method of presenting the story of a single character or a group of closely related characters in essentially chronological order, collectivism aims to portray the life of the masses and to offer a panoramic view. In literary practice, this means fusing as many different stories as possible and advancing them simultaneously, to create a general impression of varied yet typical experience and to provide a general understanding of what the whole signifies. But if collectivism offers writers a means of dealing with multiple issues, it also presents problems for those who, while exploiting the advantages of this technique, nonetheless wish to achieve a unified narrative effect and to evoke a coherent emotional response in the reader.

The nature of Herbst's subject matter helped her overcome most of these difficulties because she structured her collective trilogy around the experiences of one family. Since the members of this family wander so much and attempt so many ventures, she could distribute her narrative over different periods and geographical areas and still have a unified point of reference. By locating in each generation several characters whose lives sum up one or more of the outstanding developments of their epoch, she could make this family's experiences representative of the movement and aspirations of the American people as a whole. By stressing similarities between the ideas and experiences of members of different generations, she could illustrate the tenacity of certain attitudes and problems. And finally, by permitting each generation to carry with it the memory of those who came before and to participate in the hardships of those still living, she could effectively rely on this family to provide emotional continuity across all three books.

Yet she still had to confront the challenge posed by the absence of a controlling point of view, a difficulty she overcame by juxtaposing with the chronological present short inserted passages set in a future time. Because they foreshadow events to come, these inserts help keep the experiences of the central family in line with the overall development of American society; since they comment ironically on the action of the chronicle, they emphasize injustices of the capitalistic system. Moreover, they suggest that capitalism is moving inevitably toward disintegration and that protest is the logical outcome of decades of social and economic abuse.

Insofar as Herbst's trilogy deals with the impact of external forces on individual fates and with the larger pattern of interrelated lives, it belongs to that strong tradition of prose fiction that has its concrete and evident foundations in history and society. This tradition includes writers as varied as Stendhal, Balzac, Dickens, and Tolstoy—to name only some authors whom Herbst said she favored. Such novelists deal with individuals in their social existence, view reality as something that can be given expressive form in fiction, and more often than not charge their books with the social, economic, and intellectual history of their times. Their most common themes are those relating to change, particularly to the problems arising from evolving or disintegrating social patterns, to conflict between established and developing modes of behavior, and to shifts in mental attitude. Many of them, intent on portraying a "whole" world, employ the conventions of panoramic social fiction, and all write from some kind of recognizable moral or ethical standpoint.

Herbst's trilogy also has roots in the politically conscious radical novel of the 1930s. Sometimes referred to as "proletarian," a term the author disliked intensely because she deemed it narrow, this type of novel differs from traditional social fiction in that it is written from a revolutionary point of view and tends to have as its central protagonists members of the working class. Alternatively, as Walter Rideout notes in *The Radical Novel in the United States 1900–1954,* such novels deal with the middle class in decay and utilize "the theme of revolutionary development in some characters as a contrast to a narrative of disintegration."[4] To this group belong James T. Farrell's Studs Lonigan trilogy and Josephine Herbst's three novels about the Trexler-Wendel family. Other elements that relate Herbst's trilogy to this tradition are its ironic treatment of the American Dream, its ample sociological observation, and its incorporation of such characteristic motifs as strikes, hunger, and the drought of the Dust Bowl years.

Pity Is Not Enough

Pity Is Not Enough (1933) traces the experiences of the Trexler family from the time of the Civil War to the turn of the century. The narrative does not move straightforwardly along nor does it follow a strictly chronological order. The chronicle consists of a series of scattered episodes, some dealing with the major protagonists, others with the reactions of their relatives as news of their experiences reaches them at home. These episodes are then set against the inserts, in which the Trexler family's history is retraced and the life of another generation summarily sketched. This method of composition, through the broken continuity of the story line, which weaves back and forth from character to character and from generation to generation, produces a complex narrative pattern that only gradually yields its full significance.

The bulk of the family chronicle focuses on Joe Trexler who in 1868, thoroughly imbued with Horatio Alger ideals, leaves his poverty-stricken family in Philadelphia and sets out in search of a better life. Shortly after his arrival in Atlanta, Georgia, with an ease that surpasses his own optimism, he lands a job as a clerk in the local office of the Atlanta & Western Railroad. Dazzled by the atmosphere of lucrative economic opportunity which surrounds him, he drifts into rascality by imitating his superiors, who are growing rich effortlessly through embezzling, bribe taking, and shady real estate deals. In this way, he enjoys two years on the crest of success, generously sharing his ill-gotten prosperity with his relatives at home.

In 1870, however, the economic and political warfare which characterized the chaotic years of the Reconstruction explodes in Atlanta in the form of a huge railroad scandal. Joe, who had played but a minor role in the colossal wrongdoings, is made the scapegoat by his former patrons and has no choice but to flee the South. Having once tasted the fruits of easy wealth, he cannot rest until he finds another shining opportunity, so he assumes the name of Victor Dorne and heads out West. In the Dakota Territories, along with a multitude of other fortune hunters, he sets to work furiously prospecting for gold. Although his mistakes in choosing false veins or those too deep to be reached with the picks and shovels of the placer miners are the same as those that sent many hapless men to their deaths, Joe, eternally optimistic about the promise of the American Dream, continues to work and to plan for the future.

After a number of fruitless years as a prospector, he pools his resources with other miners to form a cooperative but very soon Eastern capitalists buy them out and make the miners their employees. Although Joe recognizes the inevitability of this Eastern invasion, he has the feeling that he is being left behind, a sensation that proves accurate as his life continues its downward plunge. He never ceases to be haunted by the railroad scandal and on every one of his business ventures loses out to some larger operator. Thirty years go by and Joe never manages to fulfill any of his ambitions. Failure follows failure with cruel regularity until, broken by continual frustration, he dies penniless and insane.

The episodes about David Trexler, the youngest member of the family, function as a counterpoint to Joe's story. After graduating from pharmaceutical college, David briefly joins Joe in the Black Hills, but when his brother refuses to buy him a drugstore, with rancor and angry words, he heads further West. He has hardly started out on his journey when he happens on an opportunity for making money by buying flour from some soldiers, who need funds for gambling, and selling it at an exorbitant profit to starving miners. David congratulates himself on his sharp deal: "it just showed he could take care of himself. Well, if a man didn't nobody else would and it was all a question of the survival of the fittest."[5] From then on he manages to look out for himself quite successfully. He settles in Oregon, where he buys his own drugstore and invests his earnings shrewdly; later, he becomes an affluent and powerful banker but never helps out his relatives in any substantial way.

These two story lines are interspersed with episodes about other family members, each of whom lives a life stunted by the pressures of external events and by personal difficulties. The oldest Trexler son, Aaron, reluctantly takes on the burden of the family during Joe's lean years, then drifts irrevocably into indolence when his mistress dies in childbirth. Catherine, Joe's most beloved sister, dies young, collapsing under the strain of too much work and the shock of learning the extent of his guilt. After marrying Amos Wendel, Anne Trexler moves in the late 1880s to Oxtail, Iowa, where she hopes to find a better future. But she too must continue to struggle as before.

Anne and her four girls are the major figures in this volume's inserts, which refer to the early years of the twentieth century and stress the nature of the heritage passed on from one generation of Trexlers to the next. The first insert, placed at the very beginning of the book, captures Anne in the characteristic pose of transmitting her vision of Joe as handsome, kind, and generous. Anne's tales of the past seem full of adventure to her children and, as the narrator stresses, become an integral part of their formative years, for as the Wendels' lives grow drearier, Anne keeps the memory of a past importance bright for them all. Subsequent inserts continue to sketch the destiny of the Wendel family and the children's reactions to their mother's tales about her relatives. The fourth, for instance, hints at Amos Wendel's impending bankruptcy and at the children's impatience with their mother's reticence about the deaths of Joe and Catherine. Perplexed, they begin to identify economic disaster and personal tragedy with the nature of life itself; "a kind of anger mounted in them, still helpless children who did not want to die" (197). The final insert finds the two younger girls, Vicky and Rosamund, in Seattle toward the end of World War I. Life in Seattle has awakened in them sympathy for the underdog, a feeling which flares when they hear talk of a general strike. But in the meantime, for some "inscrutable" reason, their lives seem to be going to pieces. Slated to lose their jobs to returning soldiers, they too seem doomed to move about continually and to wait endlessly for better times.

A Family, A Nation

Because of the many shifts in the narrative focus and since no one character possesses the breadth of vision necessary for perceiving and expressing the nature of the world in which this family moves, the social criticism offered in *Pity Is Not Enough* emerges indirectly, as Herbst fits the Trexlers' lives into a meaningful pattern and uses both individual characters and the whole family to reflect national issues.

Throughout the chronicle the hopes and frustrations of the Trexlers are portrayed against the backdrop of an expanding, materialistic America. Among the important events and movements that affect the characters' lives are the Reconstruction, the Gold Rush, and the movement West. This background gives depth to what otherwise might have been a perplexing portrait of a peculiarly unfortunate family; it emphasizes the necessity for viewing the past critically, for it shows how the destinies of these people were shaped by forces over which they had little control. Yet this perspective is continually placed in tension with the Trexlers' almost uniform unawareness that their social and economic environment has any effect on their lives.

Optimism and an unswerving belief in the promise of incalculable wealth just over the horizon define and motivate their attitude toward life and preclude their attributing failure to anything other than personal weakness or capricious fate.

Joe's story illustrates most consistently both how external forces can influence an individual's experiences and how lack of awareness about the meaning of those events can distort and destroy life. Though forever a prey to the shifting goals of his epoch and despite his many opportunities to observe the actual workings of society, he remains strangely passive and uncritical. He never acknowledges that he got rich in the South only because he was dishonest and never realizes that other people there intentionally manipulated him so that he might eventually bear the blame for their unscrupulousness. Subsequently, as if he had learned nothing from this experience, he goes out West still believing that with work and luck he can make the leap from rags to riches, an attitude which exposes him to further failures and exploitation and makes it possible for him to be swept along helplessly by a constant stream of personal and economic problems. Only once, when he reads the words of the Haymarket anarchists just before their execution ("There will come a time when our silence will be more powerful than the voices you are strangling today"), does it dawn on him that society has played a role in his personal tragedy. But by that time he is already on the verge of insanity.

Because of his persistent illusions and occasionally illegal actions, Joe is no "hero"; but he is also much more than just the most handsome, generous, and unlucky Trexler. As a youth who dreams of a brighter future for himself and his family, as a fugitive from the law who is constantly scheming to make up for his Southern losses, and as a prospector who is always being forced to sell out at the wrong time, he embodies both the strengths and weaknesses of a booming America. His aspirations and his restlessness, his wanderings and his disasters are those of thousands of enterprising men who made possible the nation's physical and economic expansion—but who rarely found for themselves the place in the sun for which they struggled so miserably. In Joe's moral flexibility are reflected, in small ways, the self-seeking and corruption involved in two of the greatest adventures of his time, the "rebuilding" of the South and the exploration of the West. Finally, the story of his rise and fall, from the eager boy who wished to emulate Daniel Boone, "fighting and never being hurt" (7), to the empty shell of a man confined to an insane asylum, is also the story of the defeat of rugged individualism at the hands of capitalism.

By contrast, David's experiences offer a brief, harsh commentary on the myth of the self-made man. Instead of being misled by Alger's heroes and fantasizing about Daniel Boone, he takes his cue from those who would transform Darwin's biological theory of natural selection and survival of the fittest into a social philosophy, a perspective that turns out to be better suited to the social and economic climate of his times. He reflects in his behavior toward his relatives a capitalistic ethos, lacking in human compassion and values. This ethos, as expressed through David, and the faltering and corruptible idealism embodied in Joe are the chronicle's real protagonists—and in Herbst's view they are also among the forces that propelled the disintegration of America's ethical and moral ideals during the latter part of the nineteenth century.

Those portions of the inserts devoted to Anne and Amos Wendel, industrious workers whose modest dreams are shattered and whose hopes for a little help from David are never fulfilled, and who courageously adjust to poverty without ever relinquishing their pathetic but sustaining faith that sometime success will come, serve to reiterate how the shortsightedness, fatalism, and inertia of the average American citizen helped to perpetuate social and economic injustice. On the other hand, the story of their daughters' early years provides a glimpse of an evolving sense of discontent. These girls, having inherited the Trexlers' inability to understand the ironic reality of the American dream as it applies to them, initially react with pity to their mother's tales about Joe and the other unfortunate members of her family. But after they experience troubles firsthand and feel that their lives are plunging toward defeat, they begin to suspect that for the elder Trexlers, as for themselves, "pity is not enough." Yet, because they are young and ill-informed, they cannot test their insights fully and at the end, though angry and impatient, cannot give direction to their desire for change.

Reviewers sensed that Herbst intended *Pity Is Not Enough* to convey a broad critique of the development of American society. However, while concurring in their assessment of it as a competently written historical novel, praising in particular the author's sense of history, the credibility of her protagonists, and the appropriateness of her style in capturing their mode of thought and speech, they diverged on the question of whether she had made sufficiently evident both the implications of her narrative and her own viewpoint. Basil Davenport, for instance, admitted in the *Saturday Review of Literature* to being perplexed by a larger meaning that he sensed was present in the novel but not fully articulated:

Of the book's authenticity there can be no question; but there may be some as to its significance. It is the sort of story that Sinclair Lewis might tell for the purpose of inviting our scorn for the mean aspirations and still meaner achievements of the characters; or that Theodore Dreiser might tell to ask our pity for those people who would like to be rich and meet with poverty, who would like to be good and meet with temptation. Miss Herbst's mood seems nearer to Mr. Dreiser's, for she has more pity for her ne' er-do-well characters than most people would be generous enough to feel; yet she explicitly says in her title that pity is not enough but does not make it plain what besides pity she wishes to inspire.[6]

As if writing about an entirely different work, Horace Gregory asserted in the *New York Herald Tribune* that Herbst's family saga, besides reverberating with national history, was written with an eye on moral values in a changing society and clearly showed that "reform is not enough, nor will pity cover the naked wound."[7]

Insight into the source of such contrasting opinions was provided in the *New Masses* by Granville Hicks, one of the most prominent left-wing critics of that period. He attributed the difference in tone between this novel and those that had preceded it to Herbst's evolving sociopolitical ideas, which had brought her away from the hard, unflattering vision of the middle class typical of her earlier work toward a more militant and informed understanding of the social forces affecting average American lives. Unlike Gregory, he sensed occasional "uncertainties of attitude" in the author's presentation of her material, lapses which he believed indicated that the "readjustment" in her social theory had occurred after she had already begun to write the novel. He predicted that "when the processes of clarification, reinterpretation, and integration have gone a little further, she should place herself unmistakably in the front rank of American novelists."[8] Herbst was not happy with what she took to be the patronizing and dogmatic tone of Hicks's evaluation and responded in a symposium on Marxist criticism in which a group of authors were asked to comment on *New Masses's* reviews of their works. The essence of her reply was that she did not wish her writing to be assessed primarily according to how closely her ideological approach to story and character corresponded to a Marxist interpretation of the historical process and that she expected critics to consider aesthetic matters and to be receptive to a broad range of literary perspectives.[9]

The Executioner Waits

In *The Executioner Waits* (1934), by exploiting the collective technique with greater skill than before and by drawing freely on her recollections of the 1920s and on her experiences as a journalist in the 1930s, Herbst moves her narrative rapidly and powerfully through wartime and postwar America, constructing a rich series of episodes, each an interpretation of one facet of the life of the times. The draft, high prices, and cheap labor are some of the issues she incorporates into her story to emphasize the social tension which, as the title suggests, is ready to explode into stormy class war. Always certain of the point to be made and never letting herself be overcome by her memories, she succeeds in weaving all of her material logically and coherently into her narrative.

Although considerable attention is paid to other family members, in *The Executioner Waits* the Wendels take center stage. As the inserts in *Pity Is Not Enough* foreshadowed, after the Wendels' move to Iowa, their fortunes kept spiraling downward. Amos's farm implement business, crippled from the start by a lack of capital, fails outright in 1914. Bankruptcy humiliates him but he accepts his plight without protest and humbly takes the first of the menial jobs that will henceforth provide his living. All during his prolonged decline his wife Anne, less patiently submissive, schemes to give her girls "advantages." She cannot accomplish much but remains unalterably convinced that something will eventually turn up.

Their four daughters grow up in Iowa accustomed to a life of continual sacrifice and apprehension for the future. The elder girls, Clara and Nancy, inherit their parents' persistence in clinging to old slogans about success and try to settle down to conservative middle-class lives. The younger two, Vicky and Rosamund, instead free themselves early from worship of material success and, after attending college at great sacrifice, begin to wander in search of a place where they can live purposefully, using their learning and their vitality. As they move, shunted from one paltry job to another, they acquire social awareness.

Rosamund marries Jerry Stauffer just before he leaves for the war. When he returns they start their married life in Detroit where she assists helplessly at his disheartening reentry into civilian society. Work is scarce and no one seems interested in succoring them. Moreover, war has changed Jerry; gone are his hopefulness and his ambitions and he seems content to drift aimlessly. Defeated in their struggle to achieve economic independence, they fall back on her parents and return to Iowa where Rosamund fights against a growing sense of the futility of her life. An unplanned pregnancy augments her worries and she reluctantly resolves to have an abortion. On the evening before her operation, however, still stunned by the morass of poverty and degradation into which she has sunk, she dies in a car accident that she seems unconsciously to have willed.

After her sister's death Vicky continues to move about. Her wanderings finally take her to New York, where she falls in love with Jonathan Chance, a budding writer and insecure renegade from a wealthy middle-class background. Like Vicky, he has sought to find good work to do in the world, to meet interesting people, and to give his life significance; but because he has always been thwarted by a jealous, possessive mother and by a father who derides his aspirations, he is unstable. Realizing that none of their previous strategies for overcoming the ways of their elders have borne fruit, Vicky and he decide to begin a new life. They marry and move to rural Pennsylvania where, under her influence, he gains new insight into social problems, while she, with his support, breaks away from her family's habit of mourning for the past and resolves to do something constructive for the future. By the end of the story they are both involved in radical politics.

All this while David Trexler has continued to prosper in the far West, multiplying his capital as that region expands and reaching the apex of his career through shrewd trading during the war. But as the climactic last scene of the novel indicates, his day of reckoning is not far off. In this scene, suggestively set in a graveyard, David witnesses the burial of a murdered striker. As the dead man's friends join together in angry sorrow to pay tribute by chanting the words of Joe Hill: "Don't mourn. Organize."

David Trexler shivered on the ignored edge of the crowd but when the yellow lumps of earth began to fall he shuddered as if they were falling into his own grave upon his own unprotected flesh.

The crowd stood tight, a hard nucleus like a fist that would never open, and he looked toward it for sympathy for David Trexler . . . But it was staring at the grave and did not see him.[10]

Revolutionary Crisis

As in the previous volume, in *The Executioner Waits* analysis of the lives of members of the central family provides the basis for Herbst's social critique, allowing her to conduct her study from within the framework of society itself. The crumbling ambitions of the middle class, for example, are epitomized in Amos Wendel. Raised on a farm in Pennsylvania, he came to Iowa and got into the farm implement trade hoping to provide his family with a secure future. But all during his career farmers experience repeated crop failures and, because of unscrupulous banking policies and governmental indifference, are unable to resolve their economic difficulties. Being by nature incapable of applying capitalism's philosophy of profit at any cost and always remaining at heart a farmer, Amos sympathizes so much with his customers that he cannot scold them into payment. Every time their crops fail, he too experiences another setback and moves that much closer toward inevitable bankruptcy. The debris of bills and worries which mounts higher and higher around him becomes emblematic of the lives of a generation of farmers and small businessmen who, in an era of supposedly frenetic economic growth, failed miserably.

While the elder generation of Wendels, taught to have faith in the future despite repeated setbacks, continues to believe in the validity of the system, the young members begin to criticize the workings of capitalism, which seem to them ever more haphazard and unjust. This change of attitude finds its most decisive expression in Vicky and Jonathan Chance. Both children of the bourgeoisie, although with very different upbringings, they eventually come to a similar understanding of the world around them and desire to find a way out. At the beginning they falter and disperse their energies in private rebellions. But by the time they decide to concentrate on the immediate task of finding alternatives for capitalism and middle-class values, they are marked as ready for participation in the difficult task of reshaping American society. A careful tracing of Vicky and Jonathan's evolution toward a sense of individual identity and social goals allows the author to explain their decision to become activists—and through her depiction of them to account for the radicalization of young Americans in the late 1920s and early 1930s—as the result of a long process of self-examination and social observation, and not primarily as a response to exposure to socialist ideas.

As before, the events narrated in the chronicle are placed in historical perspective by the inserts, which in this volume anticipate the ground swell of revolt in the early years of the Depression. Instead of emerging from observations made by members of the central family as in *Pity Is Not Enough,* however, this perspective now comes from the loud protests made by discontented farmers and industrial workers during the dark days of 1932 and 1934. Unlike the Wendels in the inserts in the first book, these people are in open rebellion against capitalism. Their choric commentary is therefore more openly polemical.

Deft juxtaposition of the inserts with episodes in the chronicle highlights the social and economic abuses underlying the large-scale ferment of the Depression. "Oxtail, 1932," depicting a group of farmers planning to disrupt a mortgage foreclosure, is placed after an episode in which an International Workers of the World convention held in Oxtail is invaded by a riotous group of "patriotic" citizens backed by the local Chamber of Commerce. "Detroit, 1932," which shows workers, who have been jailed for having marched on the Ford Company, writing Communist slogans on the prison walls, follows an episode in which Amos meekly accepts a cut in pay. Building on similar contrasts, other inserts link Jerry Stauffer's difficulties as a returning veteran and Vicky and Jonathan's disillusionment with bourgeois values to the historical processes that led to the social tension of the 1930s. Other inserts in this volume recall how, during the Depression, dust storms, soil erosion, and drought transformed vast areas of rich farmland into creeping deserts. In describing such natural calamities the author does not hesitate to suggest that they are portents that, under capitalism, human life too is doomed to disintegrate.

The increased sociopolitical observation, the sharper ideological focus, and the accelerated pace of this volume seem to carry it headlong toward the climactic last scene where, amidst the tombstones of an obviously symbolic graveyard, "the executioner waits." Yet the final tone of the novel's historical analysis is not pessimistic. Although much of the story is devoted to stressing such contradictions of democratic capitalism as the perennial depression in agriculture, the implacable survival of unemployment, and serious inequities in the distribution of wealth, as well as to the tracing of individual failures, throughout the novel Herbst strongly hints at a possible social regeneration. In the chronicle, especially in those sections dealing with the political awakening of Vicky and Jonathan, she implies that out of the old order a new one is rising, while in the inserts, which stress the growth of solidarity among workers, she suggests that the Depression may act as a catalyst to bring about major social transformations. Hers was a grandiose but not entirely distorted vision of contemporary reality. By 1934, when this volume was completed, among certain sectors of the working class there were signs that a "revolution" was already in operation. To many intellectuals this trend seemed to herald the eventual emergence of a politically conscious proletariat, committed not only to achieving economic security for themselves but also to constructing a newly just and humane society for all. This sense of the end of one epoch and the complementary beginning of another informs this second volume of Herbst's trilogy.

The tone of most reviews of *The Executioner Waits* was determined by the critics' responses to the sociopolitical ideas expressed in the novel. Geoffrey Stone lamented in the *Commonweal* that "Miss Herbst always falls short of final perfection—which failure ensues from reviewing characters by way of Marxian ideals,"[11] while in the *Nation* Lionel Abel insisted she "overplayed her propagandist's hand" by choosing to focus on characters who "have hardly any emotions that are not mechanically caused by economic problems or social convention."[12] In sharp contrast, the radical activist and novelist Mary Heaton Vorse said in the *New Republic* that *The Executioner Waits* was "a rich and terrible and tender book . . . [which] should be read, for there is no doubt of its being one of the most important documents of American social life that has yet appeared."[13] And both Obed Brooks in the *New Masses* and Edwin Burgum in *Partisan Review* congratulated the author on having provided her readers with a lucid "expression of a society at a crucial point in the class struggle"[14] in "a manner appropriate to fiction as an esthetic medium."[15]

Other contemporary critics discussed the novel in the context of Herbst's earlier fiction. Horace Gregory, who had spoken well of *Pity Is Not Enough,* felt that *The Executioner Waits* established Herbst as "one of the few major novelists in America today":

Miss Herbst is . . . painting a fresco of our times . . . The large design which one saw taking form in "Pity Is Not Enough" is admirably sustained here. Her dry, hard prose is gaining cumulative power, and, as in all examples of distinctive prose style, one begins to think of it as inevitable, as indigenous to her subject matter. [16]

Praising Herbst in *The Great Tradition* (1935), Granville Hicks extended the evaluation of her development as a writer previously advanced in his review of *Pity Is Not Enough:*

From the first . . . [Herbst] was painfully aware of the spiritual bankruptcy of the lower middle class, but it was only as a revolutionary that she could understand how that bankruptcy had come about. . . . If *Pity Is Not Enough* sometimes belied the wisdom of its title, sometimes lapsed into a kind of nostalgic, almost Catheresque lingering in a simpler past, this fault vanished when the author came to write *The Executioner Waits.* . . . The warmth and color and dramatic movement that Miss Herbst so relentlessly shut out of *Nothing Is Sacred* fill the pages of *The Executioner Waits.* Understanding has banished the fear of middle class emptiness, fear that, coupled with absolute integrity, had made necessary the starkness of the earlier book. Knowing herself beyond the danger of illusion, she can write with the power she once suppressed. Insight has brought clarity, and clarity has liberated talents. [17]

Rope of Gold

The idea that a society interested primarily in material wealth and success is tremendously wasteful of human life is the dominant theme of *Rope of Gold* (1939) which, as it brings the Trexler-Wendel family saga to its conclusion, illuminates the desperation and the anger of the years between 1932 and 1937. The main representatives of the central family, Vicky and Jonathan Chance, initially go on working for the revolution, he as a grassroots organizer among ruined Pennsylvania farmers and she as a reporter specializing in strikes and the labor movement. Jonathan has been cast off by his rich industrialist father and he and his wife experience extreme poverty. Nonetheless, he remains faithful to the convictions that have led him to choose values different from those of his parents; he registers as a Communist and for several years strives to bring to his involvement in politics a fervent idealism. Unfortunately, he is ill suited for a struggle that seems to have no end and ultimately, convinced that "men like himself were doomed never to become men of action, only yearners in that direction," [18] gives up on the revolution.

Vicky, who has an intimate knowledge of what it is like to be always on the losing side, responds with greater perseverance to the difficulties inherent in revolutionary activities. Besides, she feels urged on continually by her work as a reporter, since it brings her into contact with the problems and the courage of the working class. Only at one point, when she sees Jonathan weary and realizes that their marriage is beginning to crack, does she experience a moment of hesitation. But a journalistic assignment in Cuba, where she encounters peasant rebels planning to take over a large sugar plantation, restores the strength she needs to keep from abandoning radicalism.

Chief among the non-family members in this novel is Steve Carson, a farm boy from South Dakota through whom the book registers the increasing tendency of farmers and factory workers to organize for relief, jobs, and union recognition, as well as the importance of new methods of industrial warfare such as the epochal sit-down strike. In contrast to most characters in the trilogy, Steve has always been aware of radical ideas since his father, a backwoods socialist, was an ardent supporter of the IWW. Yet not until he becomes a man does Steve fully understand the meaning of community action. In fact, the radical sentiments he inherited from his father urge him to voice his dissent openly only after one of his friends is murdered for having tried to help farmers organize. This event shocks Steve into action, and he heads for Michigan where he takes a job in an auto factory, with the specific intent of getting involved in union activities. The last scene of the novel shows him on the barricades as a strike is about to begin.

The tragedy of people living on the land is exemplified in episodes about a number of lesser characters, such as Timm Robb. Stories like his serve as a reminder that, of all the errors hidden by the apparent prosperity of the 1920s but surfacing in the 1930s to intensify the crisis, depletion of the soil was the most appalling and also the most difficult to remedy. In their struggle against this natural disaster many debt-burdened farmers like Timm lose everything through mortgage foreclosures. Their loss of property and the knowledge that there is no escaping to a fresh valley over the hill leaves them with two choices: either they migrate to the city, there to swell the ranks of the unemployed, or they stay put and allow themselves to be subsidized and continually tormented by the awareness that their land, now too arid to support even one family, had once helped feed the nation.

That the economic injustices and the social and ethical compromises inherent in the capitalistic system have finally begun to sap the lifeblood of the people is further illustrated in a myriad of sharply drawn incidents. Faith fails a minister delivering a sermon over the body of a murdered striker because "of what use to preach the Kingdom of God when the kingdom of earth was a living pit" (380); anxiety grips the owner of a once-prosperous farm forced to stand by as it is slowly, inexorably mortgaged until "every twig, every stone, bore its trace" (87); anger explodes in the businessman who thinks that he "had put everything he had, as the saying is, into one basket. And that basket proved to have a hole in the bottom" (422); desperation invades the unemployed worker who feels like a diseased man who learns that "he had escaped death only to linger for no one knows how long helpless on his spine" (226).

The problems and conflicts treated in the chronicle are given an increased sense of urgency by the inserts, now roughly contemporary with the incidents to which they are carefully juxtaposed. A number of these inserts place social protest in the 1930s in the context of the ideals on which the nation is supposed to have been built. For example, in "In Abraham's Bosom: Washington, D.C., 1932," a group of dispossessed sharecroppers addresses the statue of Lincoln: *"You told us Father Abraham that this country was dedicated to the proposition that all men are created equal. We're still waiting for the amen to that dedication"* (81). Along with scenes of domestic strife, the inserts in *Rope of Gold* also refer to sugar workers on strike in Cuba, to Italian anti-Fascists, and to the Spanish Civil War, thereby relating the action of the book to international tensions.

A Study of Erosion

Fidelity to the outcome of actual events prevented Josephine Herbst from showing in *Rope of Gold* the drastic transformation of society to which the trilogy seemed to be pointing. Indeed, the world she depicts in this novel is one in which things do not grow to fulfillment but break, decompose, or are eaten away, and people are suffocated by having to act always under such conditions of apprehension, frustration, and violence that neither hastily seized pleasures nor endurance and courage can save them from almost total misery. Undoubtedly, the author's disillusionment with developments in radical movements in the United States and abroad, her consternation at the triumph of Fascism in Spain and at the portent of an imminent world war, and her private sorrow about the disintegration of her own marriage influenced both the tone and the social view she expressed in *Rope of Gold*. Nonetheless, she did not lose sight of the major con-

cerns of her trilogy, and in her handling of the torments and deci-
sions of the American people during some of the nation's most trying
years carried her project to a moving and disturbing conclusion.

In the portraits of her minor characters she paints an impressive
panorama of proletarian figures that includes farmers who must work
day and night not only to preserve their crops from the ravages of
weather but also to diminish the burden of debt that threatens to
bury their future, and laborers who have left the farm to go to the
city where they are subjected to the alienating rhythms of the factory
and must fight for their most elemental rights. Their stories point
out symptoms of a social failure that runs deep, for they expose the
disintegration of the fabric of society and the slow and persistent erosion of life itself. They also bring to fulfillment many of the trilogy's
important motifs. Individual failures like those often illustrated in
the history of the central family have become an everyday occurrence.
The collapse of the fortunes of people like Amos Wendel is repeated
many times over as bankrupt farmers lose their homes, their land,
and the beliefs that had sustained them. Defeat through worry and
privation, the fate of young Rosamund, is now the lot of many men
and women on whose faces it is possible to read the pain and the
amazement of people frantically trying to stay alive. Finally, death
after years of frustration, such as that which took Anne Wendel, has
been translated into the living deaths of many families unable to feed
their children or to look to the future without shuddering.

For neither Vicky nor Jonathan Chance do the radical hopes that
motivated them earlier find fulfillment in the latter years of the
Depression decade. As Jonathan becomes more involved in the Communist Party, he finds himself bewildered by the rhetorical postur-
ings of his co-workers and alienated from the common people he
wishes to help; sensations like these, coupled with a loss of faith in
himself, finally make him defect from revolutionary activities. Although Vicky has a deeper understanding of her abilities and limitations as a social activist and is able to rise resolutely above the tragedy
of her failed marriage to carry out her obligations as a human being,
she too is assailed by doubts and fears. She is forced to acknowledge
that social change in America, if it is ever to occur, will come about
more slowly than she had expected. And although she feels enormous
respect for the freedom fighters who struggle valiantly at home and
abroad against social and political forces of overwhelming propor-
tions, she has strong intimations of the breakdown of international
hopes for a revolution.

In dealing with Vicky's efforts to understand what is happening in society and in her own life, Herbst achieves some of the most poised and balanced writing in her trilogy. An episode in which Vicky figures may be taken as an illustration of this achievement, as well as of the most common stylistic and structural techniques employed in this work.

This episode shows Vicky at a fund-raising banquet organized by acquaintances who have become members of an elitist revolutionary group. Among the speakers that night are an unnamed West Virginia miner who has been stricken with silicosis, and Clement Gregory, a young man of excellent social standing and financial status. The miner addresses the audience simply and directly, telling them that he will soon die but that "the day is acoming when men will think of us workers and not just the profits they can get out of us. The day is acoming when men won't be asked to give up their lives to earn their daily bread. Someday . . ." His words are barely audible above the noise of dishes and the chatter of his well-dressed audience. Moved by his talk and angry at the indifference with which it is being received, Vicky gets up to leave. But when she hears "the burst of applause [that] seemed as hateful as if it had come from some arena," she decides to listen to what Gregory has to say. Gregory speaks "with an earnestness as real as the silicosis worker's had been." He too calls for social change, and in his speech the word "America" emerges again and again "like a bright hypnotic bead dangled before their fixed eyes, and the full land, the rolling prairies, the thick forests, and the little houses dazzled the group as the familiar images were held up, one by one." Then he launches into his program for reform, that is basically a plea for a renewal of democratic capitalism because only this system, he says, can provide the mass of the nation's citizens, middle-class people like those in his audience, with the tools for fulfilling their aspirations.

Victoria moved a step forward at the unexpected words. The silicosis worker was looking at the speaker with a puzzled expression, but Gregory was sweeping on, calling for a bloodless revolution of the white-collar class to save the world from the onrush of what was happening in Germany. Students and intellectuals were urged to join forces, but with whom? The workers were not mentioned again, and in fact, the silicosis victim who had said his piece now sat like a neglected stage prop with a puzzled expression on his painfully drawn face. Bloodshed was not the answer, Gregory was saying; the answer was evolution, not revolution . . .

The silicosis victim sat ignored like a poor relative who is lucky if he finds a plate set for him at the foot of the table. A bitter loneliness for Jonathan was as real as a taste in Victoria's mouth. The need to touch something certain was as painful as a bone. . . . She could not explain that sinking of the heart, as if she were a child again at the Peavy Grand, sitting in awe before the big drop-curtain painted with mermaids and an obscene Neptune, only to have it lift upon a stage that was the same old stage, ill concealed under clumsy paper icecakes meant to beguile you into thinking Eliza was crossing an honest river.

She heard the sizzle of applause crackle around the table, then catch fire like a chain of matches. . . . Doubtless she had lost the clue to the people who were once her friends and she listened to the talk as if it came from a country whose language she was only partly familiar with. The whole world was chopped up like that, it seemed, and Jonathan's father had sent {as his Christmas gift} a goodwill basket that had only pierced their hearts.

. . . Victoria tried to remember what she had heard about Clement Gregory and struggled as if she had known him personally once long ago, finally resurrected the description someone had given her of Gregory's energies and time going into his work, his devotion, his complete giving, like a saint. . . . He had given up music for something sterner, his beliefs, and the girl in talking of him had the glowing look of a disciple. The memory only made Victoria more unhappy, as if Gregory had been completely fortified and the silicosis worker utterly abandoned. The room seemed stifling and unbearable. How were human beings to live in times so troubled, how could they love? (119–22)

From the opening lines of this episode the reader is plunged into the thoughts of Vicky Chance and continues to see and feel the episode through her. Yet, as the first sentence of the long quotation illustrates, the author also establishes distance from her character. The result is a dual point of view carried forward throughout the episode. Also evident in this excerpt are Herbst's artistry in charting the fluctuating emotions of her character and her skill in weaving together diverse impressions. Vicky's sympathy for the miner is followed by her hostility toward Gregory, then by her uncertainty about herself. Her glimpse of the miner's incredulity during Gregory's speech sparks a reminiscence about her own disillusionment with the theater as a child, while her anxiety about what the young man's plans for the future imply for the working class heightens her personal uneasiness about what is happening to her own marriage.

The fluidity of Vicky's feelings and her merging of memories with fresh impressions are reflected in Herbst's sentence structures, which rely heavily on subordination. She first presents a seminal idea or impression, then proceeds to modify or amplify it in successive clauses. In so doing she reproduces at the character level the dominant structure of her trilogy. Vicky's passing thought about the injury that her father-in-law's gift caused her and Jonathan refers to an immediately preceding episode. Her shift from that personal feeling to its wider context, from a family injustice to the injustice of a socioeconomic order, is a model of the movement in the trilogy as a whole. What began in the acute perceptions of one Midwestern woman about her own life ends in a broad portrait of American history. Herbst's most well developed literary form and structure are apparent in microcosm in such rewarding individual passages.

Finally, this episode demonstrates how Herbst develops the complexity of her character's reality since Vicky is captured as she responds to both personal and external stimuli. The author suggests her public sorrow at the plight of the worker, her intimate suffering over the dissolution of her marriage, her bewilderment at the direction taken by the radical movement, her private disillusionment at not being able to effect sweeping changes. In a few pages Herbst succeeds in communicating very richly a sense of this character's inner life and her social outlook, and in conveying a profound feeling for the pain of experience, the pathos of the human condition, and the mystery of time and memory.

Critical response to *Rope of Gold* was largely favorable. In fact, although one reviewer maintained that it wholly conformed to the conventions of proletarian fiction[19] and another was disappointed that in it Herbst had not created a central protagonist as representative as a Babbitt or a Studs Lonigan,[20] most agreed that its complex social analysis and thoughtful delineation of character made it bear "little relation to the formula-ridden novel of the proletariat"[21] and that the author's method effectively communicated her tragic vision of American life. The most perceptive comments on the novel's connections with the American literary tradition and on its artistry came from Alfred Kazin, whose remarks appeared in the *New York Herald Tribune*. Kazin related the book not only to Depression literature but also to Midwestern Realism, especially to those works that center on the frustration and failure of the American dream:

Of all the crusading novelists who started out so bravely a decade ago to create a lean, hard social fiction fit for the '30s, Josephine Herbst has not weakened. Where so many of the proletarian Homers wrote of strikes because they needed a symbol, or of factories because the machine age was news, she wrote carefully and with quiet grace of that shambling portion of the middle class which she knew, a class half out of the barn and the factory, possessive without riches, a class always in carpet slippers, hunched over the radio for the legend of hope, drifting in an endless spiral. Her books are the latest in that long line of Mid-West chronicles of failure which have joylessly hacked the Valley of Democracy. That line began with the passing of the frontier and is being toughened on the passing of the American Dream; but the material is the same, the same hungry flies buzz around the kitchen linoleum, and the Iowa or Kansas farmer droops as helplessly in Miss Herbst's novel as he drooped for Hamlin Garland or Ed Howe.[22]

His observations on its style and method were similarly informed by an awareness of both the specific literary trend to which the novel belonged and its unique character:

. . . suffering lends a certain dark music to Miss Herbst's novel. . . . [Her style] can be hard and rasping, as her inter-chapters, with their social reportage of Spain and Cuba and the Bad Lands, their interweaving of European cities and American villages prove. But what is remarkable in this writing is its delicacy and fullness, for hers is a social saga, and cities are as minor to it as men, and farmers of no more significance in it than workers. Hers is a topical history of the American land; the years are bunched together in it, and the hero is not a man but a people. It is the first collective novel in America, moreover, which is not rigid as even Dos Passos' "U.S.A." is rigid. Such sympathy as Miss Herbst has displayed is a distinction found chiefly in those novelists whose interest rarely goes beyond individual lives, and it is that distinction that has set her apart and that gives her so much promise.[23]

The Trilogy: An Assessment

The radical fiction produced by the Left in the 1930s includes a few works that are important expressions not only of the literary and intellectual culture of that decade but also of the larger tradition of social realism. The most notable of these are John Dos Passos's *U. S. A.,* James T. Farrell's *Studs Lonigan: A Trilogy,* and John Steinbeck's *The Grapes of Wrath,* writings in which the reader finds insight into both topical and enduring political, social, and economic dilemmas artfully presented in fictional forms reflective of their authors' unique perspectives on society and human nature. Most other 1930s novels colored by radicalism are deeply marred by excessive reliance on current political theories and insufficient attention to matters of craft and technique. However, as Walter Rideout has noted, some "lesser" Depression novels are still distinctive because "written by artists who had concentrated on working out methods of expressing their own experiences truthfully, yet in accordance with Marxism as they interpreted it."[24] A comparison of Herbst's trilogy with the most critically acclaimed radical novels of the Depression decade illustrates why Rideout placed this work in his list of "durable achievements" from that period.

Each of the major 1930s radical novels is, among other things, a social documentary of the times communicating the specific point of view on the American system held by its author. *U. S. A.* chronicles the history of American life in the first three decades of the twentieth century: poverty, unemployment, and the degrading mechanization of work; war, imperialism, and political repression; strikes, agitation, and revolution all come under analysis. Throughout this work, the implied moral indignation and protest of Dos Passos take the form of delineation of defeat, a constant emphasis on how capitalistic institutions, especially big business, sabotage life. *Studs Lonigan* covers major trends in the period between World War I and the early years of the Depression; included in its third and most documentary volume are the collapsed market, failing banks and businesses, strikes, unemployment, and growing left-wing unrest. In this trilogy as a whole, Farrell indicts capitalism through a detailed sociological depiction of the emptiness of lower middle-class life and by making the failures of the main character symptomatic of a more general social waste and misdirection. *The Grapes of Wrath* records such immediate calamities of the 1930s as drought conditions, economic problems, the sharecropping life, and the migration westward; that capitalism inhibits the solidarity necessary if the lives of all Americans are to be made more humane is one of the messages that clearly emerges from Steinbeck's treatment of the struggles of his central characters.

Herbst's trilogy is likewise permeated with a broad understanding of American history and conveys her radical historical interpretation. In its dramatization of some aspects of American life from 1868 to well into the 1930s, her work links the rise of the capitalistic system with the betrayal of the nation's original ideals of liberty, equality, and justice, and stresses the notion that under this system the average citizen is most likely doomed to failure. The fates of members of the Trexler-Wendel family show not only how less-acute pursuers of wealth are baffled and destroyed and potentially valid workers have their talents wasted, but also how "successful" people are corrupted personally and even those who try to devote themselves to working for social change experience both public and private defeat. These themes are reinforced by the lives of the lesser characters, which most frequently record the pathos of poverty and exhausted land, and the slow and difficult affirmation of working-class solidarity. In order to enhance her readers' awareness of the gravity of the flaws she sees in the American system, Herbst deliberately excludes from her angle of vision many positive elements of national life and consistently uses her characters' individual dramas, meaningfully interwoven with the social and economic crises of their times, to highlight the hardships faced by less fortunate members of society. Although such an approach confers on her trilogy a somber tone, for it implies reiteration of the same message in many stories of frustration and waste, it allows her to achieve an intense expression of the suffering that unjust external circumstances impose on average citizens in the United States.

In their books, Dos Passos, Farrell, and Steinbeck all adopt a bold architectural structure, an episodic presentation of their material, and a language attuned to the idiom of their characters. They depict their protagonists in a definite time and place and in complex relationships to one another, and show their destinies being shaped by their milieu and period, their particular roles in society, and the qualities of their character. To stress the failures and injustices of the American way of life without dealing excessively in ideological abstractions, these writers translate their socioeconomic themes into human terms, situating their central conflicts in the minds and hearts of their characters. Writing as modernists, they make extensive use of interior monologue, interspersed with neutral recording of dialogue and action, avoiding as far as possible direct authorial intrusion of commentary, generalization, and analysis. To this same end, Dos Passos and Steinbeck employ some innovative devices. Dos Passos uses "Newsreels"—mixtures of newspaper headlines, news stories, political speeches, advertisements, and popular songs—and "Biographies" of famous American personalities to comment indirectly on the world in which his people move; in the "Camera Eye" he traces his own political and aesthetic development. Steinbeck's "interchapters," though more poetic and rhetorical than directly documentary, provide the necessary social, economic, and historical information to insure that his readers fully comprehend the larger story of the migrants.

Herbst utilizes some similar techniques in her trilogy. She writes in the collective mode, incorporates a great many details of national life into the fabric of her narrative, uses a group of fictional characters to furnish a microcosm of society at large, develops representative scenes to underscore her social meanings, and makes her protagonists' personal problems and individual destinies reflective of significant trends. She further historicizes her narrative by alluding to actual events, referring to newspaper stories, and mentioning real people. Her inserts suggest an ethical standard for judging the action of the family chronicle. In the first volume, like Dos Passos's "Camera Eye," they offer in language that resembles stream of consciousness the re-actions of a few individuals to their family's past and to their own present circumstances; in the other volumes, her inserts are less overtly autobiographical, serving to punctuate the chronicle with de-scriptions of social and historical events presented from the stand-point of "real life" participants in those events.

Technically, Herbst's trilogy is well executed. Careful preparation for each of the episodes that make up the various narrative strands and attention to the overall pattern of the work usually allow her to develop her ideas with increasing persuasiveness, while only rarely is the flow of her narrative interrupted because she crowds it with too many details or lets incidents that should be but minor moments emerge too strongly. Although the structure of her narrative requires her to delineate her characters in an economical way, she manages to make many of them come alive as individuals because she probes their interior responses while subjecting them to the pressures of external forces. The felt experiences of her characters are rendered in language and ways of thought appropriate to them. For the most part they use a homely idiom which, no longer barren of colorful phrasing or pitched in the monotone of her previous books, rings true through-out. This language is not rich in implication because, instead of con-verting her observations into symbolic terms, she devotes her efforts to selecting the telling detail or gesture and to shaping, sometimes too painstakingly, the irony she needs to advance her ideas. This lan-guage, however, is well suited to exploring the emotional and intel-lectual meanderings of her protagonists and to reproducing the thought processes by which they link past events and impressions with those of the present. While the characters do not always realize the significance of their association of ideas, these meanings emerge clearly for the reader.

Because of such faults as occasional overcrowding, some forced writing, repetition, and somber didacticism, Herbst's trilogy lacks the impressive power of the best radical fiction of the 1930s. But it certainly deserves more attention than it has so far received, both because Herbst's thoughtful and sensitive portrayals of ordinary men and women during some very trying periods in national history extend the reader's knowledge of the past into the realms of sympathy and imagination, and because she frequently transcends the flaws which mar the work as a whole. At such points she achieves a fine balance between the formal aspects of her art and the world view she wishes to expound, channeling her anger and emotion into moving, penetrating prose, and chronicling the experiences of her characters with delicacy and compassion.

Chapter Five
Later Novels

Two of the events that led to the disintegration of the radical movement to which in different ways so many writers and intellectuals in the United States had given their allegiance during the 1930s directly affected Josephine Herbst's life and thought. One was the defeat of the Loyalists in Spain; the other was World War II. She was in Spain at the time of the Barcelona uprising, an incident which, as she would record in her memoir "The Starched Blue Sky of Spain,"[1] signaled the breakdown of unity among the forces of the Left, and with the demise of that coalition, seriously undermined the Left's possibility of winning the war. The Moscow purge trials and the Nazi-Soviet pact would follow, but for Herbst, as for some of her associates, it was the evolution of the Spanish Civil War which represented the failure of the Marxist revolution. In 1942, after several years of voluntary withdrawal from the public scene, Herbst was impelled by her concern over the holocaust of World War II to attempt another form of activism, working as a writer for the government in Washington. Because by that time radicals were being blacklisted, her gesture, as she would recall in the memoir "Yesterday's Road,"[2] ended in the humiliation of dismissal from her job.

Herbst's disillusionment with certain radical interpretations of human nature and society and her response to the tragedy of World War II were to affect the nature of her 1940s novels. *Satan's Sergeants* (1941) emphasizes the investigation of individual sensibilities rather than collective experience and, although it contains some social observation, is principally devoted to examining the consequences of personal fallibility and guilt. *Somewhere the Tempest Fell* (1947) has as its setting Chicago during World War II; against this backdrop, it focuses on a group of characters striving to understand the truth of history and the meaning of their own experiences.

Satan's Sergeants

Satan's Sergeants (1941), like all of Herbst's previous fiction, has no central protagonist or dominant narrative thread. Instead, it consists of loosely related episodes and character sketches, each told from the perspective of a different protagonist, none of whom acts as a narrator or is a disinterested participant whose angle of vision would afford a consistent point of reference. Although this kind of "collective" form is most suited to fiction dealing with social themes, it is used here largely to investigate problems of an existential nature.

The action takes place during an unspecified year in the 1930s in Merlin, a fictitious village in the enchanting hill country of Bucks County, Pennsylvania. The score of characters belong to two social groups, wealthy city folk who are newcomers to the area and poor villagers who are mainly descendants of the Pennsylvania Dutch. During the first half of the story the narrative moves along at a leisurely pace, flowing in and out of the sensibilities of the various characters, developing their attitudes toward life and toward each other, and showing them reflecting on the incidents that have shaped or scarred them. The central section of the book deals with its major event, a huge brush fire which sweeps over the hillsides and threatens the estate of Mr. Elliott, the richest man in the district; during this emergency the townspeople finally come together. In the concluding chapters the narrative again takes up its shifting focus and provides parting glances at several major characters as they try to reorganize their lives after the fire.

The novel as a whole may be read as a study of estrangement, since its protagonists are alienated from the basic sources of emotional sustenance: from the lovely natural setting in which they live but to which they have no productive relationship; from their community which has lost its original character and now exists only in name; and from each other because of individual fears and problems. Merlin's two groups of inhabitants lack close ties with the land for different reasons. The city people, who have thrown themselves energetically into landscaping projects and into remodeling old farmhouses, have failed to establish a meaningful relationship with the land because their work has not been dictated by a love of nature but only by the hope of finding in its harmonies an antidote to their private dilemmas. The futility of their efforts is illustrated by the unnamed New Yorker who:

impatient and skeptical of the future, plowed up the meadow in front of his door and at enormous expense converted that wasted land to a genteel park of giant oaks, old elms, fifty-year maples, and little apple trees that in the second season bore fruit. Birds began to nest in his trees, and on rainy days he watched the new grass between the thick trunks brighten with the mournful thought that no one really loved him.[3]

The native villagers, who over the years have been forced to abandon the once-fertile hillsides for the lowlands, "as if they were part and parcel of some vast soil migration that might carry little pebbles and particles of earth and humans alike silently to some deep river" (2), are similarly rootless. They, in fact, have come to feel like aliens in their own territory because, having lost their ancestors' land, they must hire themselves out as helpers on private estates or find employment in one of the local paper mills or porcelain works. Alienation is increased by the strong barriers between the town's two groups of residents. The natives, though grateful for the odd jobs their wealthy neighbors provide, are envious of their life style, while the rich simply make no effort to understand the problems the natives face.

As the stories of the single characters come into focus, however, it appears that class differences and estrangement from nature do not constitute the central problems in their lives but that they are instead all unhappy because of some past error, the shadow of which makes them strangers to whatever might have given meaning and purpose to their existence. This impasse is dealt with most satisfactorily in the episodes about Belle and Will Armstrong. Through flashbacks the reader learns of the experiences that haunt these characters. At a tender age Belle fell in love with Hans, a bargeman who occasionally stopped over in the boardinghouse where she worked. When Hans died in an accident on the Lehigh Canal, Belle, who kept secret the fact that she was carrying his child, married Will and promised herself that, in exchange for his giving her child a name, she would struggle bravely to make a good life for them all. Belle has never forgotten her lost lover or her unshared secrets; though outwardly tender toward her husband, she has lived with him in psychological isolation. In Will's mind, marriage to Belle was the best thing that ever happened to him; buoyed up by her apparent affection, he even found the courage to escape from Merlin and his domineering mother by going to Allentown and getting a job as a tram operator. But one day a little girl died under the wheels of his trolley and, although no one held him responsible for this tragedy, something failed deep within him and he returned home a broken man. None of Belle's urgings ever managed to break through the wall of silence behind which he hid himself or prevented him from falling back under his mother's dominance.

During the course of the story Belle and Will are shown acting out a pathetic tragedy. He insists that her son, Johnny, leave high school and go to work in a paper mill, deriving from this act of authoritarianism a renewed sense of self-importance. She longs to assert her right to help decide the boy's future, but precisely because he is her son and not Will's, she keeps silent. After Johnny is accidentally electrocuted as he operates a machine in the mill, remorse causes Will to lose touch with reality while Belle, though equally burdened with guilt feelings, wishes to go on living as before for the sake of their remaining children. Thinking to alleviate her husband's mourning and enable them to start over again, she confesses Johnny's true identity. But she errs once more, for she cannot revive Will and what she intends as a kindness serves only to increase his sense of insignificance.

Belle and Will, with their perpetually blighted aspirations, are typical of the trapped and defeated common people who have always engaged Herbst's literary sympathies most profoundly. Here, she uses them to pose, and reflect on, the question of what meaning can be found in the lives of people who are never safe from the onslaught of poverty and bad luck and who rarely receive or can give others the kind of love and understanding they need. Will, who responds to his wasted potential and dashed hopes with overwhelming pessimism, can find no solution to his suffering and dies a suicide in the freezing waters of the Lehigh Canal. Belle, in contrast, by accepting the compromises she is forced to make and by refusing to give up completely even in the most violent, harsh, and depressing situations, earns the strength and resilience that allow her not only to avoid annihilation but also to go on trusting in the future. In fact, in the closing scene of the book, as spring approaches, she takes her two small children away from Merlin, humbly hoping that the wisdom she has won through her adversities will finally help her create a better life.

Although the Armstrongs' story emerges forcefully in *Satan's Sergeants,* the novel is not primarily about them because their family tragedy is interwoven with a great deal of material concerning characters whose lives in no way overlap with theirs. Generally, these other protagonists are less fully characterized than are Belle and Will. Indeed, they tend to be presented as personifications of the spiritual paralysis that is the consequence of crucial failure in their past lives; convinced that it is too late for anything of significance to happen to them, they limit themselves to musing over their previous traumas, and in the process further curtail their emotional and spiritual development.

Jim Dowell, for example, is haunted by the memory of the execution of one of his friends for a homicide in which he, too, had been implicated but was exonerated because of his youth. So great is his obsession with this event that he cannot establish intimate ties with other people; he cannot consider anyone a friend before he has confessed his troubled past, but once having done so he is forced by his self-contempt and fear of compassion to withdraw. Similarly self-destructive is the behavior of Martha Purcell, who allows her husband, a tormented writer, to take out his frustrations on her because she is convinced that such treatment is just punishment for having wed him without love: "It was marriage she had wanted as one falls in love with a landscape and takes whatever house has been built upon it. . . . It was lack of true, deep love that was her crime and she was a prisoner of her own failure" (167).

Along with having deprived themselves of the right to form friendships and to seek rewarding emotional involvements, characters like Martha and Jim have suppressed their ability to engage in normal social relationships. This failing, common to most of the characters in this novel, is dramatically emphasized in the episodes about the fire. During the fire, at last compelled to work side by side to save Mr. Elliott's property, Merlin's lonely inhabitants feel more respect for one another than ever before. In high spirits after putting the fire out, they gather for a celebration. The party begins congenially enough but shortly, as everyone's thoughts start drifting back to their secret problems, their newfound collective harmony is fatally interrupted.

The only individual in the book who eventually breaches the walls of her self-imposed prison and through friendship manages a kind of redemption is the cultured and wealthy Mrs. Willard. For the greater part of the story her behavior indicates that she too is resigned to a small and bitter life. She accepts her loveless marriage with a petty and ineffectual man because she wed him in a moment of desperation after her beloved first husband died; she feels that, once having made a commitment to him, she has no right to ask for more. The result of this perverse attitude has been an ever-increasing sense of emptiness and alienation, which not even her move to Merlin has enabled her to outwit. Indeed, Merlin's beauty merely accentuates her awareness that her life has become a form of death:

The enchanting world seemed behind glass and the sound of birds, the smell of wood fires and, most of all, the heavenly look of animals in the fields reminded her, each day, that she must awake before it was too late. She would find herself in her coffin behind that last and fatal glass of death, if she did not waken soon. (124)

Fortunately, Mrs. Willard has one saving grace, sensibility to the problems of other people. It is this attribute that will finally permit her to break out of her isolation. In particular, her association with Belle Armstrong, the most satisfying human relationship depicted in this novel, helps her analyze her behavior more carefully. Observing Belle's grave difficulties, participating in her tragedies, and watching her being called to account for her mistakes, makes Mrs. Willard at last recognize the real source of her own guilt:

Not for her sins, but for the omission of good or evil. She had been neither saint nor sinner. She had chosen instead that blank and empty walk of nothingness. Those who had eaten the apple could at least relish their sins. They might even repent and whatever else failed them they had their true sufferings borne [*sic*] out of knowledge. Their thick rich deeds might damn them but they had never made a mock of living. (274–75)

On the strength of this insight and at the age of fifty-nine, Mrs. Willard belatedly matures and rebels. She leaves her husband, sells her house, and bids Merlin goodbye, ready to face life courageously and in search of new relationships.

The Shadow of Sin

The material of *Satan's Sergeants*—human fallibility, guilt, and alienation—might have been worked into an intensely powerful novel; this book is something less. It evoked mixed feelings in reviewers, who chose not to discuss at length its main themes but to focus their comments on identifying the relative strengths and weaknesses of the author's imaginative and technical strategies. Almost unanimously, they credited her with a fine talent for characterization, keen insight into human behavior, and a certain deftness of style, but took exception to her overall structural techniques. In a typical listing of the positive aspects of the novel, H. P. Lazarus wrote in the *Nation* "the people are real; the perceptions are acute; the observation, the mood are excellent. . . . For the truth it has, the sympathy, the deep feeling, for the daily pendulum of American family life, the book is good."[4] Characteristic objections to the author's organization of the story were summarized in the *New York Herald Tribune* by Rose

Feld, who observed "where [Herbst] can, with masterly effect, put drama into the lives of her many characters, she fails to give the book the cohesion of a dramatic core . . . The parts are good and more than good but they fail to dovetail into a magnetic whole."[5]

As critics pointed out, the narrative lines in this novel are neither organically related to one another nor linked by a line of action that progressively rises to a peak or at some point shows a complex of character forces impinging on each other in a key scene that fulfills them and rounds out their meaning. It would appear that Herbst made a further unsuccessful attempt to join her stories together by imposing on them a mythic framework. She parallels Merlin to an Eden in decay, a once-beautiful earthly paradise that has for its old and new inhabitants been figuratively transformed into an inferno by their own behavior and that during the fire literally takes on a hellish aspect. Besides hinting that all of her characters are in one way or another "satan's sergeants," responsible for bringing sorrow into their own lives and the lives of others, she sometimes has them use biblical references in describing their own experiences, as, for example, when Mrs. Willard recalls an incident from her youth that signifies for her the moment she was "pitched out of Paradise." Yet because the author introduces the myth of the Fall only occasionally and fails to make its presence felt throughout the narrative, she is not able to make it sustain the burden of thematic resolution which she seems to have wished to impose on it. This weakness, like the structural disunity noted by critics, cannot be outweighed even by the considerable sympathy and insight with which she delineates her individual protagonists.

Somewhere the Tempest Fell

The question of identity, especially the way in which time and memory, as well as individual and collective behavior, shape human destiny, dominates Josephine Herbst's final novel, *Somewhere the Tempest Fell* (1947). She develops this theme in an intricate network of very complicated stories about characters who, almost without exception, are experiencing existential crises and are plagued by a sense of displacement. The author writes perceptively about her characters' inward unhappiness, effectively transmits their mood of defeat and disillusion, and makes the reader privy to their thoughts and psychological weaknesses. Regrettably, since no single plot element or explicably philosophical viewpoint unifies the various narrative strands, which are instead loosely linked together by the similarity of the protagonists' emotional states, this novel too remains primarily a gallery of individual portraits.

The most promising of Herbst's character studies in *Somewhere the Tempest Fell* deals with Adam Snow, a man who, because of past personal choices and his responses to the events of history, feels himself hanging on at the margins of his social and human community. After years of living in Italy, Adam, a middle-aged writer who has enjoyed fame and fortune by turning out mystery stories under the pen name of George Wand, returned to America upon the outbreak of World War II and settled in Chicago. Since that move he has been in the throes of a grave crisis which touches on his social commitment, his professional life, and his interpersonal relationships.

The opening of the novel discloses Adam reexamining his life in Italy, where he had won the confidence of several members of the anti-Fascist underground because of the liberal ideas he expressed in private conversations and his occasional gifts of money and small favors that helped some of their comrades escape arrest. At the time he had congratulated himself on his discreet, ethical behavior. Since returning to America, however, he has been possessed by the suspicion that he used his timid support of the partisan cause as a means of concealing his moral cowardice. Indirectly, the reader learns that he never exposed himself to physical danger, or made financial contributions which in any way altered his standard of living, or even took time out from his work on the George Wand series to write about what was happening around him. To evade having to assume the heavy burden of remorse that acknowledgment of such a pervasive lack of action would entail, Adam chooses to dwell on a single incident in which he behaved in a reprehensible manner—the fleeting moments during which by shouting a greeting to Pietro, a partisan leader traveling incognito in Milan, he attracted the attention of Mussolini's police, who then arrested the partisan. Adam has grown so obsessed with this incident that one day on the streets of Chicago he thinks he sees another Italian acquaintance, a mysterious figure named Zabo, who threatens him on account of his actions in Milan. From then on, both his memory of Pietro and his fantasies about Zabo become a means of camouflaging his more general feelings of guilt at always having retreated from active social engagement. Equally self-delusive in an unconscious way is Adam's plan to return to Italy after the war to help organize relief work and to write about efforts to rebuild the nation, as expiation for having betrayed Pietro.

This plan, which helps sustain him during the few weeks the novel covers, crumbles when on the last day of the story he learns that Rome has been liberated. Only then does he realize that the plan is inappropriate, not only because, having always held himself aloof from social strife, he would most likely not be able to engage himself in it now, but also because the plan is based more on a desire to re-establish self-esteem and moral equilibrium than on true political commitment.

Dissatisfaction with the nature of his artistic endeavors also contributes to Adam's crisis. As a struggling young writer he had hoped to produce something of high artistic value. In need of money, however, he started publishing stories in slick magazines; it was a short step to the invention of George Wand and the possibility of economic security. Adam had always intended to return to more demanding writing, but like so many popular authors he became caught up in his easy success as George Wand and so kept postponing his "important" books. Regretting that he has no specific identity as a writer, he decides to drop the George Wand series and to create a novel that reflects what he considers to have been his youthful potential. Yet every time he sits down to work, he finds himself falling back into his outworn themes, characters, and style and at the end is left wondering whether he cannot make an artistic breakthrough now because he never really had superior talent or because he did not develop that talent slowly and diligently during the years he had given himself over to George Wand.

Similarly problematic is Adam's emotional life. Despite marriage to Frieda, an attractive American widow he met in Italy, and the birth of two children who are almost grown, he has never felt emotionally fulfilled. This is not because his family have failed to offer him love but because he has lived in emotional stagnation, never having overcome the loss of Lucia, a girl he courted in San Francisco before he was drafted into World War I and whom he could not locate when he returned. For most of his life Adam has nourished his secret hurt. His wife also has a private burden of sorrow and guilt. Her previous marriage had so disintegrated that she wished her husband would disappear from her life; ironically, he drowned in a boating accident that she inadvertently caused. Toward the end of the novel Adam's wife reveals to him the circumstances of her first husband's death. After her confession Adam also speaks openly to her, admitting that he has always let his memory of Lucia cloud their marriage.

Their mutual recognition of each other's problems and of the wastefulness of mourning eternally for the past finally introduces intimacy and compassion into their relationship and suggests that perhaps they will be able to establish close ties.

As the author delineates Adam's multifaceted dilemma in the opening chapters, she lays the premises for a story that investigates such complex matters, all related to the larger question of identity, as the relationship of the individual to history, human imperfection and its moral and political implications, the question of personal responsibility as opposed to determinism, and ways to come to terms with social and private guilt. But after raising these complex issues, she does not then subject them to a penetrating analysis. Thus, in the closing chapters, as Adam comes to partial compromises about his social and private behavior, the reader, having been unable to follow all the stages of his quest for truth, does not understand the emotional and intellectual changes that have prepared him for the deeper self-understanding that makes these compromises possible.

What takes the place of a thorough investigation and demonstration of Adam's situation are numerous studies of other characters. To name only a few, these include Ada Brady, Harry Light, and Ralph Johns. Given the fact that almost equal portions of the action are set in the homes of Ada Brady and Adam Snow and because of the similarity of these characters' names, the reader is led to expect that Ada's story will in some way mirror Adam's. Such balancing occurs only to the extent that she too is experiencing an identity crisis and is disturbed by complications from the past. Ada, a thirty-three-year-old divorcée, is trying to overcome a sense of guilt about the breakup of her marriage and to cling to youth. For Ada, youth is represented by Chicago's bohemian culture and in particular by a very unstable jazz pianist named Lonnie Redmond. To strengthen her ties to him, she decides to transform the basement of her home into an after-hours club for him and his musician friends. But Lonnie has no intention of becoming permanently involved with her and flees Chicago. Another set of problems is introduced into Ada's story by Henry Rodney, an aging, well-to-do family friend who agrees to finance her project to remodel her basement because he views involvement in her life as a means of renewing his own youth. In return for his help, he demands that she treat him like a suitor. Many pages are devoted to demonstrating how these three troubled individuals manipulate one another and to the frustrations they experience as they try to force

each other to fill the terrible emotional voids in their lives. At the
end, each one is in more or less the same situation as at the beginning: Ada, still feeling that she has lost contact with the world
around her; Henry, hoping to restore his sense of possibility by continuing to play benefactor to her; Lonnie, unable or unwilling to
make any efforts to control his destiny.

Harry Light and Ralph Johns, even more effectively than Ada
Brady, could have been used by the author as counterweights to
Adam Snow. Part of Adam's crisis can be attributed to his not having
taken part in the social and political conflicts of the 1930s, while
Harry and Ralph both exemplify the dilemmas the shifting forces of
history created in the 1940s for people who had previously been social
activists, especially disillusionment with ideology and politics and
fear of not being able to cast aside the darkness of historical chaos.
As a Communist organizer, Harry had pinned his hopes for mankind
on a socialist revolution but, with the crushing events that closed the
1930s and with the outbreak of war, saw the world of his political
assumptions go out of existence. He now lives without any sustaining
beliefs, haunted by remembered fragments of past hopes:

Names, faces, bits of song, phrases . . . throwing him backward to the days
of his early youth when the name of Joe Hill had been like a banner in the
sky. "Don't mourn, organize," Joe had said, but who was organizing and
for what? The whole world was an organized camp, but for death not for
living. He tried to console himself by the thought that great things would
come out of the war but fear constricted his very heart. How could pitiful
wrongs ever be righted? Where would the barricades ever be raised against
the now stern enemies of men in the sky? It all sounded old-fashioned,
hopelessly dated and he stood, like an old actor, with the stage empty, the
audience departed, the myth he was to have lived by—*from each according to
his ability, to each according to his need*—still fluttering persistently in his
heart.[6]

Although Ralph, a gifted historian and journalist, did not take part
in any organized leftist movement in the 1930s, he had traveled ex-
tensively through Hitler's Germany and in other European countries
and had reported from the battlefields of Spain during the Civil War.
In his journalism he had tried to tell America what was happening
abroad and to warn of the approaching catastrophe:

He had warned stop Japan in the early days of Manchuria, stop Italy, stop
Hitler, stop Franco in Spain, but the traffic had roared past the uplifted

hands of the volunteer Boy Scouts. Then he had stopped yelling Stop, frozen in doubt as to how to stop whom, terrorized by the vision of a momentum that might have astronomical dimensions, that might begin in one place and end unpredictably somewhere else. (21)

Ralph's faith in the power of words has degenerated into sterile cynicism and he is in the process of becoming apolitical. In fact, whenever he realizes that he is speaking or thinking "with something of the thrilling audacity with which he used to summarize history when he believed that certain events and certain conditions prognosticated other events and conditions, with the element of progress the inevitable medium of the change desired" (133), he stops himself short, preferring to "abandon the superficial political, historical sphere" for a discussion of "generic conditions imposed by laws to which, as yet, we have no clue . . . to the catastrophic disasters which make terror the basis of the human totality" (136). Unfortunately, the signs of awareness of the plight of radical American intellectuals and activists in the 1940s that these two characters so poignantly suggest remain little more than signs, for neither Harry nor Ralph is dramatically absorbed into the life of the novel.

A Literary Imagination in Crisis

Dissatisfaction with Herbst's loose narrative form dominated the few reviews of *Somewhere the Tempest Fell*. Critics Diana Trilling, Howard Mumford Jones, and Richard Sullivan shared a high regard for the substance of the novel, calling the author "a writer of power" for her "inexhaustible" imaginative energy, "complicated" honesty, and "zest for experience." But, for different reasons, all of them thought the book lacked a principle of control. For Trilling, this weakness derived chiefly from Herbst's admirable attempt to write unselfconsciously about a myriad of lives:

Throughout her story Miss Herbst is present only in such light as is reflected from her characters. . . . *Somewhere The Tempest Fell* proceeds, that is, from an attitude toward novel-writing which I so much favor that I could passionately wish that . . . Miss Herbst had not also refused the necessary discipline of all good art; that in accepting the happy mess of life she had not herself produced something of a mess; and that in giving her characters the license to be free she had not also given them the gift of being more compelling. [7]

Jones was instead convinced that the sprawling structure of the novel indicated that the author had fallen victim to the "fallacy" of "the refusal of the story":

There is no portion . . . that cannot be justified as writing and as insight. But the total impact of "Somewhere The Tempest Fell" is one of confusion. The spotlight shifts so many times, the illumination falls so sharply upon so many personalities, things, problems, emotions, relations, that the eye dazzles and tires, the mind longs for sparer diet. . . . These infinite riches . . . ought somehow to be canalized and controlled.[8]

Approaching the issue of the diffusiveness of the novel from yet another perspective, Sullivan argued it was a logical consequence of the nature of Herbst's prose:

Taken word by word, or sentence by sentence, this prose exhibits a distinguished lucidity. It seems at once both solid and pure, when read in short passages. But as it proceeds, as part succeeds part, and shift follows shift, as the reader is abruptly transferred from one time and place to another, and from the mind of one character suddenly into the mind of another, as fact is surrounded by rich remembrance, and action is wrapped in long, beautifully phrased commentary, and characters are swathed in precise, unhurried analysis—the texture of the prose becomes too complex, and behind the involved organization of the writing the people and the events grow dimmed and secondary.

The question, then, is simply that old one of how hard a reader may justifiably be expected to work over a piece of fiction which, when read slowly and carefully examined, reveals rewarding compensations. "Somewhere The Tempest Fell" is a sound and deliberate, scrupulous and valid novel. Yet it is difficult.[9]

Each of these sensitive analyses points in its own way to the conclusion that in *Somewhere the Tempest Fell* Herbst failed to manage the problem of scale. She introduces Adam Snow's personality and dilemmas with such care that the reader expects the whole novel to turn on him. But just as Adam begins to react to his problems, his story starts losing its impact as the author introduces other protagonists in episodes and character sketches of almost equal intensity and detail. Insofar as these other characters are grappling with complications from their early lives and desperately seeking a new point of departure, and to the extent that their narratives elaborate on the theme of the loss of identity, they could have been accepted as complements to

Adam's story. Yet in their portraits, too, Herbst creates and then frustrates the expectation of exhaustive presentation. Before any one of them can be perceived as a fully realized individual the author whisks the reader off to consider another portrait. This device widens the scope of the novel, but it also gravely diffuses reader interest. The narrative point of view continues to move quickly and loosely from person to person, with little regard for the values of a controlled narrative perspective. The resulting structure of discrete incidents and memories never merges into a cohesive, organized whole.

Yet in her novels of the 1920s and of the 1930s Josephine Herbst was able to handle with artistry and skill the architectonics of decentralized structure, patiently accumulating all the details and facts needed to depict social conditions accurately, studying the ways external forces operated on her characters, and shifting perspective frequently to reveal their lives and private dilemmas from their own points of view. That the stories in *Somewhere the Tempest Fell* are not woven into a unified narrative fabric, therefore, cannot be fully explained only in technical terms. The artistic limitations of this novel are probably also related to a failure of vision, in particular to Herbst's inability to resolve the problem of linking the inner world of her characters' individual sensibilities with the outer world of their collective social experiences. A well-defined view of society and human nature, in fact, is what gives unity to novels like *Nothing Is Sacred* and the trilogy. Each of the five important narrative strands in *Nothing Is Sacred,* for example, places in meaningful tension the personal limitations and social conditioning that affects each character's life; considered together, the stories of the five main characters offer a general critique of middle-class values in the 1920s. In the trilogy, with a much larger cast of characters and a wealth of social detail, the author similarly succeeds in giving each of the narratives of her major protagonists a sense of completeness in terms both of individual psychology and of the actions in which the characters are involved. At the same time, she uses them all to develop an analysis and interpretation of American society that reflects her particular and discernible point of view.

In *Somewhere the Tempest Fell* the one character in whose story both personal and external factors play a part, Adam Snow, seems to have been insufficiently conceived, defined, and placed by the author. Indeed, from the start the reader is more likely to be struck by his personal problems than by their public reverberations; in the end, Adam is shown resolving with a degree of success only one of his private difficulties, his relationship with his wife. The other people in the book are caught, like Ada Brady, in very intimate dilemmas, or, like Ralph Johns, in situations primarily linked to history. No balanced design holds these two types of narratives together. The characters act out their stories against the backdrop of Chicago in the summer of 1943, during the massive social and political confusion of World War II. Intermittently, they discuss the war and the story ends with a reference to the liberation of Rome. But, with few exceptions, Herbst does not show how the pressures of war have been influential in her characters' lives.

In defense of the author, it can perhaps be said that her book accurately reflects the difficulties faced by writers in the 1940s who tried to make any even remotely definitive statements about the meaning of the life of the individual in a world of unprecedented complexity. Earlier in the twentieth century, writers who retained a belief in the scrutability of historical forces could explore the place of individual action amidst the pressures of sweeping public events in literary frameworks that conveyed the impression of being capacious enough to encompass a "whole" world. Now, history seemed to have no controls and no inner logic to be perceived and expressed; the search for a fictional and personal order based on it had become a troubling and inconclusive endeavor. This is not to imply that the weaknesses of *Somewhere the Tempest Fell* are to be taken as the measure of Herbst's achievement; it is only to suggest one further source of those failings and one probable reason why this book was to be her last attempt to illuminate through fiction the large social, political, and cultural conditions of her contemporary reality. The directions her work took in the 1950s and the 1960s are the subject of the next two chapters.

Chapter Six

A Biography, a Novella, and a Gathering of Stories

Seven years after her last novel appeared Josephine Herbst published *New Green World* (1954) and "Hunter of Doves" (1954), works which show that despite personal and professional setbacks she was determined to continue to grow as a writer. In *New Green World,* looking back at eighteenth-century America and admirably re-creating the atmosphere of wonder and discovery that characterized the beginnings of the science of natural history, she offers a delicate biographical interpretation of John Bartram, the first native-born American botanist, and follows the fortunes of his son William Bartram, botanist, ornithologist, and artist. At first glance seeming to be an unusual undertaking for an author with her interests, this book is in fact another chapter in her lifelong investigation of the development of American society, complementing her novels and memoirs. "Hunter of Doves," the only completed portion of a projected series of stories about artists who were her friends, is a finely crafted novella inspired by her recollections of Nathanael West. This work occupies a crucial position in the evolution of her literary career. It shows her drawing on skills developed in earlier experiences with the short fiction form to overcome the technical weaknesses that detracted from her last novels and writing in a newly complex and poetic style; since it has as its subject matter the attempt to deal with the past as it exists in memory, it fictively anticipates the composition of her memoirs.

New Green World

Love of nature and admiration for people who sought not to exploit the American wilderness but to understand and preserve it led Herbst to write about John and William Bartram and sustained her during the laborious research that this task required. To these commemorative motivations was added the didactic intent of reminding her contemporaries of the intellectual, physical, and spiritual heritage these two men represent. As she writes:

I began to be interested in the Bartrams, father and son, because of a flower in my Pennsylvania garden but I stayed with them through NEW GREEN WORLD because they were so alive, though long dead. Living for more than themselves, they were unafraid of new horizons and so their story breaks through parochial notions of our historical past to reach around the world. Long neglected, the Bartrams broke ground for Audubon, Thoreau and many others. The plants they rescued from the wilderness survive; the vitality of their search speaks to us today.[1]

Unmistakably the work of an accomplished novelist of social fiction, the biography is a blending of history and personal narrative in which the emphasis falls almost equally on two points: the lives of the central figures and the period in which they lived. Facts and incidents from the Bartrams' lives and quotations from their books and letters are presented and interpreted to highlight fully and interestingly many important aspects of their character and habits of mind. Brief discussions of their friends, colleagues, and patrons and of the social, political, and scientific institutions of their times place them firmly in the context of their epoch. The book also evokes a sense of the enormously rich natural world of eighteenth-century America and offers a commentary on the twentieth century's wilderness, in which human beings wander divorced from nature.

The John Bartram in Herbst's account is botany's servant and master, unafraid of humble tasks and yet imbued with the courage and initiative to attempt a rare enterprise. Untrained as a naturalist but possessing the aptitudes of a scholar and an extraordinary energy, he took the whole of the American frontier as his laboratory, carrying out with resolute skill his responsibilities as botanist and explorer, sending great shipments of specimens abroad, and corresponding about his findings with virtually all the distinguished naturalists of his day. At home on his farm in Pennsylvania, a large tract of land which he rescued from swamp along the Schuylkill River, he established the first botanic garden in America that contained both native and exotic plants and conducted what were probably the first experiments in hybridizing on the American continent. In discussing these activities Herbst notes with admiration that in all of them Bartram acquired his knowledge and achieved his goals directly through his own efforts. As she puts it, "botany came to Bartram through his eyes and hands as he ploughed the fields or searched the woods for wild honey. . . . Nature thrust at him and he thrust back, making roots and seeds, rocks and moisture yield the yeast of his living" (3, 21).

To place John Bartram in relationship to the scientific Enlightenment, Herbst examines his travel journals, *Observations on the Inhabitants, Climate, Soil, etc. . . . made by John Bartram in his travels from Pensilvania . . . to Lake Ontario* (1751) and *A Description of East Florida, with a journal kept by John Bartram* (1766), both of which deal with journeys he undertook for the British government. To that same end, she draws on his celebrated correspondence with another member of that little coterie of men who devoted their lives to what was then known as natural history, the prosperous London merchant and ardent amateur botanist Peter Collinson. She finds that Bartram's books, written to communicate a vision of the abundant riches of the frontier and with an eye toward their social uses, reveal both a wondering excitement at the revelations of untamed nature and a typical eighteenth-century urge to catalog and impose order on nature's bounty. His letters, she stresses, testify to his convictions that nature was a storehouse of beautiful and useful beings created for man by a beneficent deity and that his scientific inquiries in the American forest offered unique opportunities to reflect on the wonders of creation at work. These letters also serve to help her trace the evolution of his ideas about progress. They demonstrate that for most of his life he expressed the conventional Enlightenment belief that an expanding knowledge of the world would help increase the happiness and comfort of all mankind, but that in his later years, as he watched the settlers plunder his beloved green world, he began to voice a suspicion that the gains of progress might ultimately sever man from nature.

As Herbst shows, William Bartram received a solid preparation in the field of botany through study of the plants in the family garden and by accompanying his father on several of his expeditions; from childhood he revealed himself to be a gifted artist of the natural world. Nevertheless, because he was too gentle to oppose his father's well-meaning but misplaced efforts to install him in some "secure" livelihood, he was able to begin focusing his knowledge and talents exclusively on the plant and animal life of the frontier only in 1773 when Dr. John Fothergill, owner of one of the largest botanic gardens in England, agreed to finance a journey of botanical exploration into the southeastern colonies in exchange for specimens and drawings. William Bartram returned to Pennsylvania in 1778 to settle on the family estate where for the rest of his life he cared for the Bartram garden and put his learning at the service of all who applied to him. The chief cause of his fame is his account of the five years he spent wandering in the southern wilderness, *Travels Through North and South Carolina, Georgia, East and West Florida* (1791). A work of substantial literary merit, this book made a strong impression on the Romantic poets of England and France who drew on it in their descriptions of the New World.

In presenting William Bartram, Herbst emphasizes those aspects of his personality and outlook that differ from his father's and relates the contrasts between father and son to some of the shifts in attitude that accompanied the transition from the Age of Reason to the Age of Romanticism. She stresses how William, adding to his father's scientific curiosity an artist's sensibility to form and color, entered the wilderness not only in search of information and specimens but also to revel in a sensuous appreciation of its beauties, and how by mingling beliefs from the Scientific Deism which he absorbed from his father with a pantheistic philosophy, he developed a sympathy with nature that made him closer in spirit to the Romantics than to his own contemporaries. Comparing their publications, she notes that John Bartram, writing helpfully for his patrons and fellow botanists, adopted a laconic style that was a product of the Quaker tradition of plain speech reinforced by the spirit of scientific objectivity; William, whose book was unjustly criticized when it appeared for containing more poetry than science and would have its most appreciative audience in a generation younger than the author's, wrote as both scientific observer and conscious artist. She agrees with other scholars that William diverged most from his father in regard to the Indians. She describes as his major failing the elder man's insistence that the Indian was the most fearful aspect of nature to be found on the continent. Her comments on William's respect for the Indians, evident in the many pages of his book devoted to studying their customs and culture, show how it reflected his Quaker background but also bordered on a Rousseauistic appreciation of noble savagery.

Despite their differences, Herbst believes that John and William Bartram shared certain important characteristics as individuals. Because each made his work an exaltation of life itself, neither ever doubted his sense of purpose or lost his feeling of being connected to the world around him; both started out and always remained "whole men confronting a whole world" (1). The Bartrams also seem to her to have had essentially the same dream of America. They viewed it as a place where people might finally learn to establish a harmonious balance between the social and the natural, using the products of their surroundings wisely to satisfy their proper material and spiritual needs. Had more of the early settlers found this vision congenial, she suggests, America might have developed into a very different nation.

"Hunter of Doves"

The novella "Hunter of Doves" (1954) centers on a woman's recollections of her youthful friendship with a novelist who died many years before and through these memories on a reexamination of some of her past experiences; the author herself and Nathanael West are clearly discernible in the two protagonists, Mrs. Heath, the woman who remembers, and Noel Bartram, her novelist friend. Narrated in the third person from the perspective of Mrs. Heath, the story unfolds in three moments. The first of these, which poses Mrs. Heath with the task of interpreting Noel Bartram, takes place while she is being interviewed by Timothy Comfort, a young literary critic who intends to write an introduction to a volume of Bartram's collected novels and who hopes that she will agree to discuss Bartram with him. Mrs. Heath does not wish to get involved in Comfort's project, not only because she doubts his ability to penetrate the complexities of Bartram's works and life, but also because she has always refrained from dwelling on that particular part of her past since it corresponds to the period when her marriage failed. Thus, during the interview she maintains a remote attitude toward her visitor, responding cryptically to his questions and indulging in private memories of Bartram and unspoken evaluations of his fiction. The long central section of "Hunter of Doves" focuses on Mrs. Heath in solitude as, having resolved to overcome her fears and to surrender to the flow of her memories, she reconsiders the past. In this part of the story, by summoning back into her consciousness Noel Bartram, members of his family, her former husband Lucas, and herself as a younger woman, and by reexamining scenes, incidents, and conversations which took place more than twenty years earlier, she starts to give to her memories a coherent and significant pattern. In the closing scene she meets Comfort in New York. While he discusses the progress he has made on his introduction to Bartram's novels, she again assumes a detached attitude and continues sifting through her memories. At the end she does not disclose anything of what she has thought but merely encourages Comfort to continue his work.

A brief comparison of "Hunter of Doves" with an essay about West which Herbst published in 1961 highlights the degree to which she drew on her interpretations of West's fiction and on the factual circumstances of her friendship with him to write her story. The essay opens with a paragraph that concisely summarizes what in Herbst's view are the essential characteristics of West's writings:

[West's] novels are dark parables embodying West's vision of what it means to be a human being in this world. There are no heroes. . . . Whether they are housewives or whores, Mexicans or cowboys, Alger boys struggling upward, journalists or would-be actors, the people in West's novels are all bit players in a violent modern drama of impersonal collective forces. There are no big shots; no tycoons; no one can be said to be in the money. The only valid currency is suffering. The paraphernalia of suffering surrounds the sufferers and streams from the air. The vibrations surge from irrational impulses from within, powerful and inexplicable forces from without. If there is love it is etched in the acid of what love is not. If there is courage it is no more than the persistence of human beings to endure in spite of all.[2]

West's concern with a troubled and violent world, the brilliant strokes with which he creates his truncated characters, and his sharp insight into the ways subconscious urges can distort or destroy life are the principal ideas on which Herbst elaborates in the rest of her essay. To them she adds a few comments on West's style and his relationship to the literary and artistic scene of his times, as well as a discussion of the affinities and differences between his fiction and the work of Fyodor Dostoevski, his favorite author. Many of these same ideas were anticipated in "Hunter of Doves," where Mrs. Heath observes, for example, that Bartram's created world has the nightmare quality of an intense dream, is populated by characters who are memorable not as living individuals but as "masks" through whom the author speaks his terrible messages, and offers an even darker view of life than can be found in Dostoevski, with whom he, like West, was obsessed. Indeed, so insightful and expertly explained are the ideas about West's art presented as Mrs. Heath's comments on Noel Bartram in "Hunter of Doves" that some of them have been quoted and elaborated on by subsequent critics in their studies of West.[3]

In the essay Herbst also provides a roughly chronological detailing
of incidents from West's life during the years of her friendship with
him. She recalls that she and John Herrmann met West in the fall of
1932 when he was manager of the Sutton Hotel in New York City
and that, on hearing West complain that his job was making it im-
possible for him to complete *Miss Lonelyhearts,* they pressed him to
take a leave of absence and to dedicate himself entirely to finishing
his novel. Encouraged by their enthusiasm, he first agreed to visit
them in Erwinna, Pennsylvania, and subsequently to rent a room in
nearby Frenchtown, New Jersey, where in a burst of creative energy
he soon completed his manuscript. West, with his sister Laura and
her husband S. J. Perelman, then bought a home in Bucks County
and, during a year of frequent meetings, Herbst and Herrmann grew
as close to him as his innate reserve would allow. In 1933, for economic reasons and at the urging of his relatives, West accepted an
offer to become a scriptwriter in Hollywood where he worked unhappily for several months before returning to Bucks County. He re-
sumed his friendship with Herbst and her husband and worked on *A
Cool Million* until nagging financial difficulties again sent him to Hollywood and out of the orbit of their lives. In 1939 he was killed in
an auto accident. All of these facts correspond faithfully to the general biographical information about Noel Bartram contained in Mrs.
Heath's reveries in Herbst's novella.

"Hunter of Doves" is, however, more than simply a fictionalized
version of Herbst's later critical essay on Nathanael West. The most
essential factor distinguishing the novella from the essay is Mrs.
Heath, in whose mind the action of "Hunter of Doves" resides and
is given meaning, and for whom the process of remembering Noel
Bartram is also a struggle to order her subjective reality, to apply insight to experience, and to repossess part of her past. The other major
source of difference between the two pieces is the emphasis given in
each to certain contents. In particular, in the essay it is mentioned
only in passing that the man West—cordial, humorous, and aloof—
was difficult to reconcile with his writings, which are marked by a
deep sense of anguish and by despair about the condition of the
world; nor is much weight given to Herbst's recollections of West's
close but difficult relationship with his family or his love of hunting.
These memories, conditioned by the contours of Mrs. Heath's sensibility and subjected to the kind of imaginative reevaluation that can
only exist in creative literature, assume central importance in
"Hunter of Doves."

According to Mrs. Heath, the despair that Bartram wrote into his fiction derived in part from his characteristically intense responses to such frustrating external circumstances as having to deal with family opposition to his choice of a career that in no way assured financial success and having to work at jobs like managing a hotel and being a scriptwriter in Hollywood which, because unsuited to his character and temperament, created in him a state of psychological tension. That despair, she believes, was also an expression of an intensely private dilemma: his dangerously consuming affection for his sister Nora and his resulting conviction that her husband (and his best friend) Joel Baker was only a surrogate for himself.

Mrs. Heath has always been aware that Bartram's practical difficulties provided him with inspiration for some of his most accomplished work. She recalls, for example, that when she read the novel he had written while working at the hotel, she found its characters to be stunning transformations of the portraits he had sketched for her of the people who lodged there and its major action to be illustrative of the kind of torment and violence he had attributed to their lives. It is only in retrospect, however, that she understands how the emphasis placed in his books on waking nightmares and grotesque suffering relates to his problems with Nora and Joel. By carefully reexamining the few glimpses she was given into the true nature of Bartram's ties to these two people, she sees that his dealings with them gave him his strong grasp of antirational behavior and of its importance in human affairs; his highly original literary talent had enabled him to utilize that knowledge in his fiction without ever betraying its autobiographical source.

As Mrs. Heath's reminiscences about Bartram's love of hunting unfold it becomes clear that for Bartram himself this activity was a way of transcending his frustrations and his obsessions. By escaping into the woods, he could disengage himself from the pressures of the business world, forget his fears of never becoming a successful writer, and leave behind the pain and guilt of his secret love. For Mrs. Heath, in the course of the story, his hunting assumes a much larger significance. Through meditation on incidents that indicate that Bartram refused to orient his ways of dealing with the problems of his life toward the easiest solutions but rather sought to defend himself in his own way at all costs and against all opposition, she comes to view his hunting symbolically. It becomes for her a reenactment on the physical level of his unending psychic quest to individuate and to pursue what he valued most. Accordingly, the beautiful, elusive wild doves which were his favorite prey are the emblem of his aspirations. Seen in this light, Bartram's hunting was no escape. Instead, it was a means of returning him to himself and of putting him in touch with one of the essential characteristics of the human spirit: a striving for fulfillment that remains undiminished in spite of all obstacles.

Mrs. Heath's enlarged understanding of Bartram as a writer and her transformation of him into a "Hunter of Doves" help her overcome some of the pain she still feels over his loss. Greater insight into the failure of her marriage is another result of her journey into the past. For, as she realizes at the start of the story, to remember Bartram is to remember her ex-husband Lucas Heath. The two men had at first seemed to be so alike. Both tall and soft-spoken, when they met each was at a stalemate in his literary career for particular economic and psychological difficulties and each insisted that he nonetheless wished to become a serious writer. In consequence, some of the exuberance with which Mrs. Heath had urged Bartram to leave the hotel and finish his novel derived from the hope that by encouraging him she would also help her husband begin to write again. Yet long after Bartram brought his book to life, Lucas still floundered. Mrs. Heath has always acknowledged that her inability to conceal her anger and bafflement at Lucas's failure to respond to her encouragement contributed to bringing her marriage to a close; now she finds the courage to admit to herself just how much her admiration for Bartram played a role in that breakup. It was not only that Lucas could not write that upset her; she had wished him to display the full measure of Bartram's artistic genius and his personal drive. Lucas had sensed her feelings, perhaps had shared them, and the shame had sent him away.

At the very end of "Hunter of Doves" Mrs. Heath, who up to that point has been profoundly and melancholically absorbed in her drama of memory even during her second meeting with Timothy Comfort, turns to him and with unexpected warmth wishes him good luck on the essay he is writing about Noel Bartram, adding that she now believes that her friend's works will someday receive the recognition they deserve. No other explanation is given for her change of attitude but it would seem to be due also to her having finally repossessed that part of her past that, though one of disappointment and pain, is for her of extraordinary importance and interest. In being reappraised, that past has most likely acquired some new meanings that are the product of a synthesis of what actually happened then and of how Mrs. Heath presently understands and responds to those events. But whether or not what she remembers is true or right in an absolute sense is of less importance than the fact that for her the process of reconfronting her experiences has made her own inner life more complete and more serene.

The organization of the narrative in "Hunter of Doves" appropriately stresses the personal, interior nature of Mrs. Heath's quest into the past. Aside from a few bits of dialogue during her meetings with Comfort, the story consists of her silent meditations, cast in the third person and arranged according to the inner logic that governs an individual's stream of consciousness. At the start of each scene the author provides a stimulus that initiates her character's reveries: the visit by Timothy Comfort, letters he writes to her, their meeting in New York City. Then she allows her to range freely from one remembered moment to another, punctuating the flow of her ideas with references to the fluctuating state of her emotions and showing how she pauses occasionally to return to the present to readjust her perspective.

Throughout, the past does not come to Mrs. Heath as a series of facts in clear relationship; because "the years could not be recalled in their continuous sequence of day by day but were enclosed in a memory of a single sun-parched afternoon or some cool evening,"[4] her quest engages not only her memory but also her imagination. At the outset Mrs. Heath worries about whether she can carry out her quest competently, expressing her fears indirectly in the form of uncertainty about Timothy Comfort's critical acumen:

she could not imagine turning an unfamiliar into Klee's studio, for instance, and expecting such a person, however well intentioned, to make anything of the table littered with shells, a skate's egg, bits of dried moss, a piece of coral, fragments of textiles. The inner watching that was the core of Klee's work would be concealed from such an eye, no matter how electrically awake. The inner necessity that was the way out for Klee, needed inner watching to detect, and a gift, yes, a gift was also needed for the detection. (312)

The subsequent evolution of the story, a gradual and sustained tracing of how Mrs. Heath reviews and reinterprets her earlier experiences and feelings, shows that her fears were unfounded; it also firmly establishes that her efforts to give shape and significance to the discontinuous, fragmented material of her memories constitutes the novella's subject matter as much as the memories themselves.

The style of "Hunter of Doves," reflecting the way Mrs. Heath's mind operates and the subtle complexity of the action in which she is engaged, is more allusive than that in any of Herbst's previous work. Mrs. Heath's reference to Paul Klee, for instance, functions on several levels. It describes the plight of Timothy Comfort as he approaches the life and fiction of Noel Bartram; it draws a telling analogy between Klee's paintings and Bartram's writings, both reflective of an acute and complicated sensibility and constructed out of bits of reality arranged in startling new patterns; and it implies that if Mrs. Heath is to detect a coherent significance in her past she must bring to bear on her recollections all her powers of synthesis and interpretation. Precisely because Mrs. Heath's main task in the novella is to discover and create meaning where she at first sees only chaos, "Hunter of Doves" alternates realistic narration of past experiences with poetic renderings of her moments of luminous insight. A key example of this technique is the section that begins and ends with her recalling how Bartram behaved the day after his engagement party, a celebration that soured because of his problematic relationship with Nora and Joel. In the midst of a fairly straightforward account of what happened that day Mrs. Heath has the vision of Bartram in the guise of hunter that marks the culmination of her transformation of him into a figure of mythic proportion:

Bartram stood at the top [of a hill behind Mrs. Heath's home] with his figure in a flowing contour against the sky. The very outline of his body was fluid and fluid the movement of his arm as he moved it briefly with the gun. He was standing, resting the gun now against the ground, and he seemed to be looking down the slope that led to the wide river. He might be painted flat, she thought, like the figures in the ancient caves, where each separate object is clear but connected too with other strange things, one thing springing from another, contradictory things fusing, all united by the charge of life, surging with it, fluctuating at the edges, never still. And if she had suddenly seen a wonder-beast join him on the hillside, half-lion, half-goat, she would not have been amazed . . . at that moment, he seemed secure in an old, old world, storming with eternal oppositions beyond mental reconciliation. He stood there, appeased and safe, and for the moment at least, she knew that he must feel the night roll off like a sickness. She could see it from afar. The next moment, he disappeared, sudden as a diver, over the rim of the hill. He seemed to have fallen into a sea of air. (331)

Because the leisured elegance evident in this passage is character-istic of the novella as a whole, it is unfortunate that "Hunter of Doves," which had a very limited audience, did not help regain a reputation for its author and that she was unable to complete and publish other works of fiction written in a similar manner. Yet the novella remains an important work in her canon. Demonstrating the degree to which she recaptured and refined her narrative skills after her unsuccessful novels of the 1940s, it brings form and content into a delicately balanced and effective relationship; though it lacks the sociological and historical substance of most of her earlier writings, it confronts with clarity of vision several other of her major themes, in particular, the individual in self-conflict, how to establish a per-sonal identity, and the effect of time and memory on human con-sciousness. In writing this novella Herbst undertook one arduous quest into her past; the preparation of her memoirs would require many such journeys. Moreover, as she gave shape to her memoirs, she would be able to measure how she expressed her ideas against the high standard she had achieved in "Hunter of Doves."

Short Stories

During the three decades between 1923, when her earliest profes-sional publication, the story "The Elegant Mr. Gason," appeared in the *Smart Set,* and 1954, when "Hunter of Doves" was printed in *Bot-teghe Oscure,* Josephine Herbst published more than two dozen works of short fiction in a variety of prominent commercial periodicals and significant "little" magazines. As was the case with her novels, she seems to have found a congenial narrative mode for her short stories at the beginning of her career and she varied it very little in the en-suing years. Her tales uniformly emphasize character portraiture rather than plot development, have a relatively uncomplicated struc-ture, and are told in a simple, concise language by a concealed nar-rator. Many of them have the flavor of a reminiscence, the form that several explicitly take, and all are pervaded with touches of irony eased by a note of compassion. Generally centered on women, the sto-ries are concerned with ordinary emotional and psychological reali-ties, in particular, with the quality of relationships between people, with the importance and difficulty of learning to understand oneself, and with self-deception.

Some of the characters and themes that would become typical of Herbst's stories were already taking shape in the three poems and one prose-poem she contributed in 1917 and 1918 to the *Occident*, the student literary magazine at the University of California at Berkeley. These works in fact consider the psychological strictures confining women both in and outside marriage. The woman in the prose-poem "Kept-Cat" is admiring the carefully chosen yellows and golds of her living room when she notices how nicely her amber knitting needles and her blond hair "toned gently into the scheme"; feeling pleased instead of disturbed at having literally become part of her home furnishing, she looks forward to sharing her observation with her husband. By contrast, the young woman in "Pagan" knows she cannot "fit to a ruled pattern" of domestic ways and races from her small town toward a lover who represents a life of art and romance. Again employing images of entrapment, in the ironically titled "Star-Dust" Herbst reveals a self-liberated woman's ambivalent attitude toward her freedom. She breaks away from marriage because the oppressive monotony of its "swish of night circles" and "creak of day circles" is grinding her dreams to dust, only to find that once on her own she still feels "the sting of wheels" and envies her husband's new wife. The last of these poems, "Silences," contains one of the author's most dreary portraits of matrimony. Its central figure, Hester, in an effort not to repeat her mother's mistake in marrying a man so uncommunicative he made her forget the pleasures of gaiety, chooses a fun loving husband and for a while enjoys days that "seemed little dream voices." But after discovering her husband's infidelity and giving birth to a strangely taciturn baby, she resigns herself to living, like her mother, in a silence broken only by the sounds of her kitchen chores.[5]

The female perspectives on love and marriage examined in these poems are extended in Herbst's first short stories, "The Elegant Mr. Gason" and "Happy Birthday!", published in the *Smart Set* in 1923.[6] These well-conceived works owe their effectiveness to the author's already skillful ability to render the intimate thoughts and feelings of her protagonists in a third-person narrative voice that is limited to but not completely identified with their consciousness. The sympathetically portrayed heroine of "The Elegant Mr. Gason" is Emma Bowen, a middle-aged woman who, though in love with her husband and satisfied with marriage and motherhood, cherishes fond memories of a youthful romance with John Gason. From her reminiscences, evoked by her daughter's humorous recounting of a chance meeting with Gason's son, emerges a conventionally romantic image of two young lovers exploring books, music, and the beauty of nature. What is unusual in the tale is the insight that over the years this image has been for Emma not a source of self-pity for lost happiness but rather a properly-valued reminder of those qualities, interests, and aspirations that are still an integral part of her personality, even if they cannot often be expressed in her prosaically real life. In "Happy Birthday!" Herbst instead depicts a protagonist who probably will never be able to overcome her disillusionment in love. Caroline, a lonely young woman with fewer inner resources than Emma, decides to express her secret affection for a man who has been kind to her by buying him an expensive present. At his birthday party, however, meeting his fiancée breaks Caroline's dreams and leaves her feeling a silly, frustrated woman consigned to a drab existence.

Herbst's ability to observe and record her characters and their actions with a realism that is coolly compassionate is particularly evident in her stories about the causes and consequences of marital disharmony. "Dry Sunday in Connecticut," published in the *American Mercury* in 1926, has as its major theme the tensions experienced by women who accommodate themselves to relationships that restrain their pursuit of self-development. The chief characters are Mr. and Mrs. Sherman, aspiring young writers who pride themselves on having established a marriage between equals and who have moved from New York to rural Connecticut so they can devote themselves to perfecting their craft. Yet they have not been very productive in their endeavors because Mr. Sherman is constantly inviting people over for the explicit purpose of getting drunk. By focusing primarily on Mrs. Sherman's mind and emotions as she copes with one of her husband's interminable drinking parties, the narrative reveals that she responds to his insensitivity to her wishes and needs with passive hostility. In the presence of his guests she acts the part of gracious hostess and understanding wife who recognizes his desire for human contact; in the privacy of her upstairs room she expresses to herself her anger at her self-effacement. Her one openly rebellious gesture, throwing a brass candlestick to the floor toward the close of the tale, ends in frustration, for "the noise downstairs went on just the same . . . No one heard her."[7]

Eight years later and again for the *American Mercury,* Herbst returned to the marriage question in "A Man of Steel."[8] Here the husband, Ernest Truax, is shown to be a pretentious man whose feelings toward his wife, Miranda, are best described as falsely solicitous, while she emerges as a sensitive woman uncertain of her own worth because her two previous marriages ended in divorce. After a series of self-deprecating and self-defeating hesitations, Miranda overcomes her fear of admitting yet another failure and of being on her own once more, and decides to leave Ernest. The short concluding scene, quite different in tone from the end of "Dry Sunday in Connecticut" where Mrs. Sherman's inner conflict remains unresolved, finds Miranda alone in her new apartment dispelling all her sad memories with a cup of strong black coffee. She has survived intact and can now get down to the business of living her own life. The divergent endings of these stories reflect the same changes in Herbst's view of human nature as those documented in her novels. Indeed, "Dry Sunday in Connecticut" looks forward to *Nothing Is Sacred* (1928) in its emphasis on the individual's entrapment in circumstance and personality while "A Man of Steel" echoes one motif of *The Executioner Waits* (1934), the possibility of making a new start in life.

Containing little overt action but much scrutiny of psychological motivations and responses, both "The Golden Egg" and "As a Fair Young Girl," which appeared in *Scribner's Magazine* in 1930, attempt to highlight the contradictions and disillusionment inherent in the single woman's search for emotional fulfillment in the modern world. "The Golden Egg" focuses on three small-town Midwestern women whose quests take distinct directions. The rebellious Ada Madders heads for New York where she associates with the sophisticated, sexually emancipated youth of the early 1920s; her friend Sylvia Gregory, after being thwarted in a love relationship with a man her family feels is beneath her social status, retreats into an unwanted celibacy; Sylvia's sister Ethel goes through a phase of intense involvement in religion, then marries Gerald Turner. Largely through description of correspondence between Ada and Ethel, with the latter occasionally providing information about Sylvia, the story comments on the relative happiness of married and unmarried women. Neither woman stresses the more painful aspects of the life-style she has chosen, for Ethel's letters are full of pious homilies on femininity, motherhood, and the connubial state, while Ada's express her motivated rejection of conventional values and finally reveal that she has had a number of love affairs. As time goes by Ada begins to share Ethel's letters with her New York acquaintances, who laughingly dub Ethel "the goose that lays the golden egg"; in turn, as Ada learns from Gerald when he comes to New York on a business trip, her letters have been read by him to his office buddies, who are intrigued by "the honest way she wrote about things."[9] The story ends on an ambivalent note, with Ada reading a letter about Ethel's Christmas holidays with her children and about Sylvia's newly acquired interest in music and feeling that, after all, her own life has not turned out as she had hoped. "The Golden Egg" is only partially successful as an exploration of womanhood in transition, for if the author's presentation of Ada can be said to comment intelligently on certain important aspects of the sexual revolution of the 1920s, her depiction of Ethel's complexity is limited to hinting at her envy of Ada's freedom, while Sylvia is a shadowy figure whose deepest reactions to her destiny remain hidden both from the other characters and from the reader.

Also set in the early 1920s, "As a Fair Young Girl" examines the similar psychological subterfuges adopted by two otherwise very different women in order to evade having to define themselves as temporarily or permanently without male partners. The young Cora Jeffers uses her meager savings to travel to Berlin to be with Boyd Johnson, a reporter with whom she has a tenuous relationship. When he heads for Constantinople, whimsically leaving her in charge of his extra clothing, she stays on in Berlin alone for several months and then moves to Italy where she settles in a pension in Florence. On impulse, she lets it be believed that Boyd's clothes belong to her fiancé killed in the Great War. This tale wins her the sympathy of the middle-aged Miss Campbell, who confides her own "romantic secret": that in an earlier life she had had a thwarted love affair with Lorenzo de Medici. Using Miss Campbell's influence as an excuse to indulge herself, Cora too starts living in a world of fantasy populated by real and imagined ex-lovers until an incident that shows the full extent of Miss Campbell's melancholic loneliness frightens Cora into facing up to reality and planning for her future. Most praiseworthy for its subtle probing into Cora's feelings and state of mind, the story falters in its study of Miss Campbell, who simply seems to be a stereotypically frustrated and slightly unbalanced "old maid."[10]

More sympathetic portraits of older women are to be found in a pair of stories published in *Tomorrow* in 1949, both of which make extensive use of flashback to provide an overview of the major events, relationships, and disappointments in these women's lives. Amy Garden, on whom the narrative of "The Last Word" centers, never actually appears as a character. Prior to the action, she was evicted from her home by her former husband who, as the story opens, is going with his new wife Elsie to inspect the house before putting it up for sale. He enters alone to find that it has not been changed except for the addition of a faint drawing by Amy on the kitchen wall depicting the two of them sitting in a café in Paris on the day they met. This sketch makes his mind crowd with memories of their life together and almost brings him to admit that in leaving her he abandoned a part of himself. But he is able to shake off his melancholy when he remembers that he left her because she displayed too many of the strengths he lacked:

With a woman like that a man simply had to walk out to save his life. . . . Oh, there was no beating her. There was no forgetting she hadn't crumpled up or died or even married again but had just gone on being herself. And it was that which was hardest to bear. He couldn't bear it now. He could hear the very echo of her voice in the walls of the house and of course it was exactly what she had wanted. Anything for the last word! Anything to make him feel humiliated and a fool.[11]

Then he rushes out to Elsie, Amy's opposite in talent and temperament. Somewhat more somber in tone, "A Summer With Yorick" offers an appealing character study of an ailing older woman who during a seaside vacation finds that each event she witnesses or hears about sends her back in time to review one of her earlier experiences. At first perplexed by her inability to keep her mind on the present, she gradually learns to value her memories and to use them as a retrospective reevaluation of her life as it draws to a close.[12]

When not writing about women and their emotional and existential dilemmas, Herbst most frequently turned her attention either to the desiccated lives of lower middle-class Americans or to radical politics. Typical of the former group, "A New Break," written for *Scribner's Magazine* in 1931, stresses in precise detail the material and spiritual deprivation of three protagonists: an unstable young man with a record as a petty criminal who deludes himself into thinking he can become famous by writing the definitive novel about prison life; his ailing wife, who uses her illness as justification for failing to act to change what is amiss in her marriage; and her domineering mother, who has never understood that her emotional alienation from those around her is the major cause of her unhappiness.[13] Published in *This Quarter* in 1931, "I Hear You, Mr. and Mrs. Brown" similarly focuses on a family in which each member is beset by a different form of psychological paralysis. Specifically, the mother is sexually

frustrated; the father conceals his weak character under an authoritar-
ian facade; the son despises his own submissiveness but lacks the
courage to rebel openly; the daughter, after attempting one autono-
mous act, settles into inertia and allows her father to maneuver her
into an unpromising marriage.[14] Both of these "slice of life" glimpses
into middle-class families display Herbst's acuteness in discerning the
selfishness and falsehood that often determine an individual's behavior
and in examining the complex mechanisms governing interpersonal
relations. In neither story, however, does she manage to suggest that
her material encloses a significance that extends beyond itself or to
arouse her reader's lasting concern for her characters.

With the excellent "The Enemy" as the notable exception,
Herbst's stories with radical themes tend to be slender accomplishments. "The Governor Does Not Come" (*Magazine,* 1934), for example, is simply a straightforward illustration of the estrangement of
Mexican peasants from officials of their national government,[15] while
"The Golden Harvest" (*Partisan Review and Anvil,* 1936) has such an
uncertain focus that the reader is never quite sure whether it is a
modest rendering of a subject dealt with by many writers in the
1930s, the political "conversion" of one member of the proletariat, or
whether it is a parody of that very topic.[16]

Sociopolitical concerns are instead sensitively and intelligently han-
dled in "The Enemy," which appeared in *Partisan Review* in 1936.[17]
Set in Havana during the general strike of 1935, this story has as its
central character Mrs. Sidney, a journalist with left-wing connections
who has been sent to Cuba on a dangerous assignment. Overtly, she
is to function as a reporter interested in interviewing the owners and
managers of the major sugar companies to learn their ideas about
workers' discontent; covertly, she is to act as liason between the in-
surrectionists and an unnamed revolutionary political group in the
United States. Because of her respectable manners and self-control,
Mrs. Sidney has been able to speak with and deceive many officials of
the sugar industry. Winning the confidence of the other side has been
much harder; in fact, only the hope that she might really be able to
evoke sympathy for their cause has made them extend her a qualified
trust. While it has, of course, been easy for her to dismiss the pater-
nalistic, capitalistic views of the sugar industrialists, she has been tormented by her mixed responses to the arguments advanced by the
revolutionaries, who, ill informed about the economic and political
situation internationally, seem convinced that once their story is

known, workers the world over will rally to their defense. She would like to share their optimism but experience has made her cynical.

Besides having to deal with ideological anxieties, Mrs. Sidney is trying to reconcile herself to the recent emotional trauma of her husband's abandonment of her for another woman. Throughout most of the story, she fights to keep her mind on her political mission and to push aside the temptation to give herself over to her private sorrow. But toward the end, alone in her hotel room, she is overcome by heartache. Then, remembering the larger tragedy that surrounds her, she resolves to place her obligations to others above her personal needs. Based on Herbst's experiences as a reporter, reflecting the disintegration of her marriage to John Herrmann, and indicative of her point of view on the radical movement toward the end of the Depression decade, "The Enemy" is Herbst's most impressive short story. It reproduces on a small scale some of the vision and artistry that inform her major works from and about the 1930s, the Trexler-Wendel trilogy and her memoirs.

Chapter Seven
Memoirs and Journalism

In her three memoirs, "A Year of Disgrace" (1961), "The Starched Blue Sky of Spain" (1960), and "Yesterday's Road" (1968), Josephine Herbst neither offers a rigorously factual reconstruction of the past nor forges new myths but, as is appropriate to a memoirist, strives to communicate a sense of lived experience seen in retrospect. These memoirs are, in fact, artfully written, reflective, and interpretive recreations of some of the significant events that shaped her thought, her activities, and her writing in the years between the two world wars. In each, using her own life as a focal point, she reviews a period of particular crisis, charts the public and private circumstances that helped determine her behavior, refers to the attitudes and reactions of some of her associates, and highlights incidents and events that in her estimation delineate the confines of that period.

"A Year of Disgrace"

"A Year of Disgrace" (1961) places in the context of the times some of Herbst's experiences in Connecticut, New York, and Maine from the fall of 1925 to the late summer of 1927. In 1925 she and John Herrmann had moved to New Preston, Connecticut, where at first, in the isolation of a farmhouse in winter, they had devoted themselves to the preparation of some manuscripts and then, during a fleeting spring and summer, had talked, relaxed, and enjoyed nature in the company of other artists and writers, including Katherine Anne Porter, Ernest Stock, and Nathan Asch. She describes that period of camaraderie as a sort of sabbatical from direct involvement in literary, political, and social movements, calling it "an interlude of time as clear and uncertain as a drop of water. . . . Where were the sources of energy: in work, in love, in the ground itself? We could try them all, reaching into the bin that seemed to have no bottom."[1] With the first frosts of 1926 everyone was on the move, and Herbst and Herrmann were among those who headed back to New York. They took the first available jobs and settled in a run-down apartment

on lower Fifth Avenue to wait for their recently completed manuscripts to be accepted and to seek more contact with other literary
hopefuls. Their circle of friends soon numbered many who were to
become special lights in America's literary world: Allen Tate, Caroline Gordon, Hart Crane, Robert Penn Warren, and Malcolm Cowley. All refugees from a provincial America that they despised for its
puritanism and lack of interest in the creative arts, these writers were
attempting to define themselves as intellectuals and to adjust to the
strain of living in a changing postwar society.

The muted sociopolitical concerns of the majority of these artists
and intellectuals, Herbst observes, was one expression of their disillusionment with the way history and society had evolved since World
War I. Progressivism, which had motivated the previous generation
to link art and social reform, had failed; the Great War, justified
with the rhetoric of a "war for democracy," had ended in the debacle
of Versailles; idealism in politics had given way to an urge toward
"normalcy." Consequently, sharing a disaffection with ideology, the
new generation were for the most part political negativists who acted
out their rebellion against the status quo by mocking the absurdities
of political leaders, attacking the manners of the middle class, and
adopting a joyfully disenchanted and emancipated life style. Such behavior, she stresses, was a justifiable and vital response to contemporary society:

> The youthful juices had neither jellied nor atrophied and if some of the
> young played with the recklessness of a gambler, with no more of a stake
> than talent and a fanatic's will, if the risks were high, what did you lose?
> The bottom had dropped out of the old world and it was a truism that the
> "old men had not only bungled the peace" but had screwed up the works.
> . . . Disenchantment was not only a necessity, it was a joy. . . .
> We knew we were in a period of evolution and called it a transitional
> time. What period is not in transition? We named it as if it had never hap-
> pened before, feeling ourselves actors in a rare moment, caught in a situa-
> tion that would require not only flexibility but intensity of purpose. (140–
> 41)

Herbst's recollections of her first few months in New York provide
her with the occasion to comment favorably on the stimulating cultural atmosphere of the mid–1920s and indirectly to express her re-
gret at its passing. "The era that gave the Model-T Ford to the
farmers," she writes, also "opened the world to its literary young on

a scale never before ventured and not equaled since" (142). Not only did the little magazines solicit and print every type of innovative writing but even some commercial publishing houses made it their business to keep up on the latest literary developments and the most promising authors. Similarly, no body of élite critics passed chilling judgments on new work and, in the absence of tight literary coteries, among practicing writers the most diverse ideas could mingle and grow in "a sort of ridiculous, gorgeous, open-house limbo" (144). For the time being, it did not matter that some literary experiments were as obscure as a Chinese ideograph, for contact with any art that overturned the outmoded ideas of beauty associated with the bourgeoisie meant being in touch with an emerging aesthetic and preparing oneself to contribute to its development.

For a while Herbst shared many of the dominant ideas and attitudes of the New York literary community. But as 1927, her "year of disgrace," wore on she started to detect in some avant-garde art "a scatterbrained diffusiveness . . . that aroused suspicion" and began to ask herself if "modernity was becoming a cult" (148). Such thoughts were to help shape her reactions to some important public and private experiences over the next few months. In April, for example, just before leaving for a vacation in Maine, she and Herrmann and almost every other prominent and would-be promoter of new art forms attended the Carnegie Hall premier of George Antheil's *Ballet-Mécanique*, considered one of the most important cultural events of the decade. First performed in 1924, Antheil's work observed certain Cubist principles of the day and, in reaction to the romantic music of the earlier twentieth century, used percussion and mechanical sound sources for its structural effects. Knowledgeable critics had described it as a visual-aural sensation, suggesting primitive and mechanical erotics. Yet, try as she might, that night in Carnegie Hall, Herbst could not force herself to be as enthusiastic about the maddening music as her friends, for it seemed to her to be an invitation to regress to barbarism:

What did the music mean? I longed to be moved as all our friends seemed to be, including John, but it seemed to me that I heard no more than a hallelujah to the very forces I feared. My longing for a still small voice, for a spokesman not for the crash of breakers on the rock but for the currents, down under, that no eye could see, made me feel alone, but not an alien, and I looked at John, too, coldly, as one who had joined forces with some mysterious enemy. Was Antheil to be the symbol of an opposition to the Philistine? In a corner of my heart a slow movement of the pulse began to turn my attention elsewhere. (150)

On the same day she attended the concert, she learned that the death sentence had been irrevocably passed on the Italian immigrant anarchists Nicola Sacco and Bartolomeo Vanzetti. To her questions about the directions being taken by some modernist experimentation were thus added intensifying anxieties about society and politics.

Through the spring and summer, however, she put all her doubts behind her as she vacationed in Wiscasset, Maine, and assisted Herrmann in readying an old ketch which they named *Josy* for a trip down the coast to New York. Toward the end of August, poised for their great adventure, they sailed out of Boothbay Harbor. But they never reached New York, for on the twenty-second of the month, while sailing through a dense fog, they decided to cut short their trip at Portland. At midnight, as Herbst and her husband sat in a diner, Sacco and Vanzetti were executed. They listened to the report on the radio, then to the Italian cook in the diner, who asked: "Electricity? Is that what it's for? Is that the thing to do? Seven years they waited. Not bad men. No. Good men" (159). Herbst admits that she cannot recall her reply, but remembers feeling that a conclusive event had occurred. Then, moving from her direct emotional response to the execution of Sacco and Vanzetti to a broader perspective, in retrospect she endows that fateful night with its full significance: as a crucial moment when external events intersected with her private world, as an experience effecting a slow and profound but also transitory change in her behavior, and as one moment in the ongoing evolution of her unpredictable existence:

So far as I am concerned, what had been the twenties ended that night. We would try to penetrate the fogs to come, to listen to the buoys, to read the charts. It would be three years before we took down a volume of *Kunstgeschichte* from our shelves to be replaced by a thin narrow volume in red, entitled *What Is To Be Done?* by V. I. Lenin. Then in a few years it would be taken down to be replaced by another. And so on.

How could I have known that night in Portland that once we had beached the *Josy* at Cohasset I would never see her again? But I never did. Years later John went to look for her, alone, and found her bashed in by a heavy tide, the planks rotted, her skeleton white as a bone. He wrote me about it. For by that time we had parted, and I no longer saw him. (160)

"The Starched Blue Sky of Spain"

"The Starched Blue Sky of Spain," (1960) Herbst's memoir about the Spanish Civil War, treats the last of her experiences as a radical activist and journalist during the Depression decade. She went to Spain to report on the war in March 1937, eight months after the outbreak of the conflict, and remained there until June. Some of the motives that had impelled her to go and some of the reasons this war became a symbol for the values and aspirations to which people like herself had given their allegiance in the 1930s are touched on early in her memoir when she writes:

I suspect that it was the question of my own fate that took me to Spain as much as it was any actual convulsion going on in that country. . . . In a certain sense I hoped to find in Spain an antidote to the poison I found in Germany, when in 1935 I went . . . [there] to write a series of articles for the *New York Post* . . . In another sense, I was probably trying to find some answers to the confusions in my own mind. The thirties had come in like a hurricane. An entire young generation had been swept up in a violent protest against the realities of events. But the answers were numbing. The slogans were pieces of twine throttling something that was struggling. Phrases like the "toiling masses" did not answer terrible questions.[2]

Thus, along with sharing the conviction that this war was probably the last chance for the triumph of a humane and democratic society in a Europe moving with terrifying swiftness toward Fascism, she had sensed that its outcome would have a profound impact on her own destiny, since the attitudes and beliefs that had shaped her sociopolitical involvement seemed to be facing an ultimate test.

While in Spain she spent most of her time either in Madrid in the company of other writers and journalists or in small towns along the central front with soldiers and Spanish peasants. Much of what she says about Madrid centers on her recollections of Ernest Hemingway and John Dos Passos in whom she discerned two distinct responses to the act of commitment in Spain. Although both men were staunch anti-Fascists with a longstanding and devoted affection for Spain and had come intending to help in the making of *The Spanish Earth*, a war-documentary film to be shown at fund-raising benefits in the United States, they were reacting to the circumstances of the war in very different ways. Hemingway, who had raised money to supply the Loyalists with ambulances and medical supplies and was daily risking his life during the filming of *The Spanish Earth*, appeared to be motivated by humanitarian impulses and at that time to be sincerely convinced that General Francisco Franco would be defeated in his attempt to overthrow the Spanish Republic. In contrast, Dos Passos displayed deep concern that ideological disputes among the various factions on the Left would undermine the Loyalist effort. This dark view was reinforced when he heard that José Robles, an old acquaintance whom he knew to be liberal and democratic, had been executed for treason by the Loyalists. For Dos Passos was certain that Robles had been a victim of the very kind of intrigue he feared pervaded Spain. Herbst, who could not stop hoping for some turn of international or local events that would make a Loyalist victory more possible, admired Hemingway's optimism. But unable to believe firmly that the Loyalists would be able to translate their lofty ideals into concrete action and triumph, she shared some of Dos Passos's pessimism.

This same ambivalence—uncertain and fearful, yet hopeful that someday, somehow, human liberty as she understood it might become a reality—is also evident in her memories of the trips she took outside Madrid to meet volunteer international soldiers and Spanish peasants. In her description of the several days she spent with members of the Abraham Lincoln Brigade at the front lines near Jarama, a scene of recent fierce fighting, Herbst stresses that while she was with them she yearned to share their revolutionary hope that owing to their efforts "*this time*, a great new world might once more have a chance" (89), but that after returning to Madrid, she again grew convinced that as long as the Western democratic governments held fast to their "infamous" nonintervention pact and watched passively while Hitler and Mussolini supplied Franco's forces with sophisticated weapons, these soldiers, armed as they were with unreliable guns and grenades, could not possibly shape the course of history. Similarly, when exposed to the spirit and courage of the Spaniards she met in the little town where *The Spanish Earth* was being filmed and to the resilience of the peasants living in the ancient caverns at Alcala de Henares, her fears of a Loyalist defeat faded momentarily into the background. They reemerged, however, when she recalled with sorrow and indignation that idealism could not prevent Franco's bombs from killing these innocent victims.

Despite the many forebodings of a final breakdown of unity on the

Left, Herbst remembers that it was with great astonishment that she listened to the news of the Barcelona uprising in May, 1937 when anarchists, communists, workers, and civil guards shot at each other from behind hastily erected barricades while the "other" war went on in the rest of the country. Without attributing full blame to any particular group, she takes her stand with those historians who see this struggle as the result of power politics and who feel that it was an act amounting to nothing less than a moral and military betrayal of the cause for which the Spanish people were fighting:

Before I left Spain the disintegration had begun with a squalid internecine brawl in Barcelona. I had never had much heart for party polemics and it was not for factionalism that I had come to Spain. I did my best to find out "the facts": I even went to Barcelona in May where barricades were still in the streets. We shall never see that kind of outmoded fighting again. No more barricades! They were even outmoded then and proved nothing. I can't say to this day what really happened in Barcelona, in all the diversity of conflicting causations, but I do know for certain that it was no anarchist plot hatched up in conjunction with Franco. If the enemies of Franco had split into groups and were killing each other, it was not because each group was not equally determined to defeat the common enemy. Was the aim of the war a revolutionary one, which would strike at the terrible wrongs which had led to the uprising, or was it a "war for democracy" which, to the intransigents, implied no more than a restoration of the *status quo*? By that time, abstractions had taken over on the Loyalist side; on Franco's side the superiority of weapons was surely winning. (80)

By diverting its energies to brawls within its own camp, the Left, she felt, had not only helped seal the outcome of this war and crush the hopes of creating an undivided society in Spain, but had also contributed to making it very unlikely that radical and liberal idealism could triumph anywhere else.

Herbst concludes her memoir by mentioning an incident that concisely sums up her state of mind during the fateful months she spent in Spain. One day, at a filling station on the road between Madrid and Valencia, she was chatting with a young Spanish soldier when a civilian came up to them and asked who she was. On being told that she was an American journalist who spoke some Spanish he joined in the conversation and when he marveled at how she seemed to understand everything that was being said, the soldier observed that not only was she *muy intelligente* but also *muy valiente*. Josephine Herbst recalls:

I was far from understanding everything. About the most important questions, at that moment, I felt sickeningly at sea. As for being *valiente*, who wasn't? If I wrote it down in my journal, it was to put heart in myself, if only to say, come now, be *muy intelligente*, be *valiente*. Just try. (117)

She was destined not to have many more opportunities to test her intelligence and courage by direct participation in current events, for because of what she had seen and felt in Spain, when she returned to the United States she gradually withdrew from all her radical activities and affiliations. Yet she never regretted having gone to Spain, for that journey brought her important though painful knowledge. Politically, it not only exposed her to the brutalities of the Civil War but also to the disheartening spectacle of bloody hostility among the very left-wing groups who were supposedly fighting for the shared aims of defeating a Fascist enemy and creating an egalitarian society. Psychologically, even as it reaffirmed her faith in "humanity" through the decency and goodness she saw in the Spanish partisans, it revealed to her that the whole issue of political involvement was becoming so extraordinarily complex that she could never again hope to draw from it any kind of personal sustenance.

"Yesterday's Road"

Although after her trip to Spain Herbst intended to dedicate herself exclusively to her fiction, when America entered World War II she tried to put her talents to work on behalf of efforts to bring this new conflict to an end by accepting a position with the Office of the Coordinator of Information in Washington, D.C. As she recalls in the memoir "Yesterday's Road" (1968), she was hired early in 1942 and assigned to the German desk of the Donovan Committee, which was responsible for preparing anti-war propaganda for broadcast overseas. Her specific duty was to help write radio scripts to be transmitted to Germany by short wave. Among the objectives that she and her colleagues were instructed to focus on was convincing German soldiers and their wives that the longer the war went on, the more likely it would be that their spouses would be unfaithful to them. As a woman, a social activist, and a former sojourner in Germany, she instinctively questioned the effectiveness of such propaganda:

Hunger would have made more sense; older Germans remembered its pangs from the First World War; younger ones from the rickety legs of kids during the inflation. But *sex*—if I knew what I was talking about, damaged goods would have more appeal than empty arms, and the women knew it, the men knew it, and would be more likely to laugh than weep at our piety. *Sex*—to *Germans* who were pulverizing Jews and politicals, by the millions.[3]

Nevertheless, her work was judged satisfactory and she was due for a promotion to the New York office or overseas when one day she was abruptly informed that she was fired. The complete motives for her dismissal were never made clear but since some of her superiors had supported Franco's regime in Spain and since many officials in Washington were then growing concerned about Communist infiltration into the government, it is likely that her anti-Fascist stand during the Spanish war and her earlier Communist sympathies each played a part. Her firing foreshadowed the kind of harassment that many liberal, radical, and left-wing individuals and groups were to experience from the mid-1940s through the mid-1950s, when fear of Communist subversion and other forms of "un-American" influences would become a sort of national neurosis.

In the first section of this memoir she describes her interrogation by the Civil Service investigators whose task was to review her credentials and decide on her reliability. The session consisted mainly of their reading to her a list of her activities during the Depression decade, beginning with her trip to Russia in 1930 and continuing through her presence in Spain in 1937. Each item on the list was presented as evidence incrementally supporting the accusation that she was a security risk. She recalls that "there were a good many of these charges, linked to the events of the thirties and the role I had played in connection with each, and, put to me in bulk, I was impressed with the record" (84). But she felt uneasy because the "charges," taken out of their historical context, seemed meaningless, and because many of the experiences that she deemed crucial to her development were being overlooked. She wondered, for example, if she could explain to the investigators how Rilke's line "Choose to be changed. With the flame be enraptured" had once ignited her passions or whether they could comprehend her emotion in Paris in 1935 when she witnessed the funeral procession for Henri Barbusse, whose antiwar novel *Le Feu* had inspired her as a college girl. As she listened to the investigators, she of course referred to none of these or to other such "irrelevant" personal experiences; but she thought back on many of them and even speculated about the kind of statement she would make about them and about her life in the 1930s if she had felt that she and her interlocutors had truly been able to communicate:

> I could remember some quoted lines from an old notebook where it is said that each man, according to his racial and social milieu and to his specific point in his individual evolution, is a kind of keyboard on which the external world plays in a certain way. All keyboards have an equal right to exist. All are equally justified. Something of the kind had even been built into our own Bill of Rights. But now these words sounded hollow, echoes from a departed summer twilight when the wooden croquet balls had jovially knocked against one another on the green lawn. In the convulsed knock of world upon world, could an individual keyboard hope to sound a single, clear, personal, or harplike note? . . .
>
> They could take *It is Reported that in Madrid, in 1937, you broadcast in behalf of the Spanish Loyalists*, turn it inside out, and find me involved in a conspiracy, where I saw only evidence of my own well-grounded reasons of the heart. Or what was I to make of the Report that I had signed a petition in 1932 protesting the violating of civil liberties in Detroit? No details were given and I couldn't remember what it had been all about. Or the one on the piece for the *New Masses* in 1935, when Batista was shooting students on the university steps, while in the mountains near Santiago peasants stood with machetes, behind virgin trees, to guard their land and what they took to be their rights from the soldiers who were mounting the slopes in obedience to commands from the sugar planters in the valley below. I no longer wrote for the *New Masses*, nor would, nor *could*. But it had served my keyboard once, as my piece had doubtless served theirs. And I stood by the substance of it, which had its own life and veracity apart from author or publication. I had only to remember the frail wishbone from a skinny chicken the mountain folk had shared with me, and which a child, who had never gone to school, had pressed into my hand at parting. . . .
>
> So I said "why do you keep saying *It is Reported* when it is a fact?" . . . [Then] I volunteered that they'd forgotten a thing or two. . . . (87–90)

Convinced that she had responded in good faith and as honestly as she had been able to the forces of history, she saw no reason to feel guilty about her behavior or her advocacy of radical and liberal causes once subsequent events made history evolve in a way that she had not foreseen. Thus, unlike such former radicals as Max Eastman, Malcolm Cowley, Joseph Freeman, Granville Hicks, and John Dos Passos, each of whom made public their anguished disenchantment and rupture with the revolutionary ideals they had once espoused, she never made any apologies for her activities, her beliefs, or her mistakes during the 1930s. To do so, she maintained, would be to betray her own self: "The experience was my own; no outsider could subtract it from my totality. Who is to rob you except yourself? The heart must weigh the stone it earns" (93).

The second section of this memoir concerns the trip she and John Herrmann took to the Soviet Union in the fall of 1930. Ever since the Russian Revolution, that country's social and economic experiments had been repeatedly described, analyzed, attacked, and defended in the American newspaper and periodical press. Moreover, some writers and intellectuals with radical leanings, like Max Eastman, Lincoln Steffens, Joseph Freeman, Theodore Dreiser, John Dos Passos, and Michael Gold, had felt the need to travel there to see the Marxist philosophy of history in operation. Few of them had come away with unqualified admiration for Soviet Communism but most remained convinced of the vitality of the Revolution and its fundamental correctness in terms of human values. Herbst went primarily as a writer, hoping to attend the Second World Plenum of the International Bureau of Revolutionary Literature to be held in Kharkov from November 6 to November 15; but since she was at that time moving into her most radical phase she was also quite naturally interested in studying the socioeconomic changes occurring in Russia. What she observed and heard during her stay did not effect a sudden and extreme transformation in her attitudes toward society and literature; in fact, on both issues her trip raised more questions than it resolved.

In Moscow, before the official delegates to the conference arrived, she learned that the people were starved for information about the outside world and that the country was not the promised land of radical dreams. During that period Herrmann stayed with a literary scholar in his tiny room and was deluged with questions about contemporary American writers and their relationship to their society, while Herbst lodged in the cramped apartment of an agronomist who wished to hear all about the lives and difficulties of American farmers. In the daytime the two of them wandered about the city looking at the empty shops and being watched by the attentive eyes of poorly dressed citizens. Finding that housing and food were scarce and luxuries almost unobtainable did not surprise Herbst for she knew that the Soviet leaders, in an effort to bring their backward country into the twentieth century, were implementing the First Five Year Plan, which promised enormous industrialization and agricultural collectivization under the direction of a central government agency. However, it did seem odd to her that the Russians she met in the early days of her visit did not speak of what the Plan foreboded but rather limited themselves to talking about problems that directly affected their everyday lives. Uncertain as to whether their reticence about the Plan was the result of ignorance or repression, she refrained from asking many questions but she listened carefully as they described their personal realities, "not making any judgments but sopping up and taking in; or tutoring my backward keyboard to new tunes. How to reconcile Rimbaud's *la Vraie Vie* with the commune" (98)?

The arrival of the rest of the delegates signaled the end of her informal interactions with the Russian people and her leisurely investigations of the city of Moscow. She and Herrmann were moved into the hotel where all the delegates were staying, were lectured endlessly on the Plan, and were taken on sightseeing tours of factories, nurseries, and communal kitchens. On the appointed day they headed for Kharkov. Herbst was dismayed to find that the important Russian writers she had hoped to meet there were conspicuous by their absence. Where were Maxim Gorki, Boris Pasternak, and Ilya Ehrenberg? "Why was it that when the Conference at Kharkov began, the General of the Red Army, Budenny, strode in like a hero, to great acclaim, but not Babel, who had ridden and fought with him? What was the cavalry without its bard, or Pushkin's statue in the square without Onegin" (100)? Moreover, as the author of *Nothing Is Sacred* and *Money for Love*, two novels about the middle class, and as a woman who never felt comfortable with intellectual absolutism of any sort, she was perplexed by the nature of most of the speeches given at the conference, which announced the advent of Proletarian Literature and attacked anyone perceived as "selling out" to the bourgeoisie by writing about that social class, and which urged writers to unite against imperialist war and in defense of the Soviet Union. She did not doubt the sincerity of the lecturers and knew that to understand what was happening in Russia and to prepare herself for the years to come in the United States, she would have to revise her intellectual and emotional perspective. But she was also convinced that her reality was not the one being expressed by the speakers: "Their keyboards were struck by winds which I could not feel or respond to; dogma was to them the needed arm, not anathema. . . . I thought, something overwhelming is at stake, but what? I can't find out here" (103).

As she looks back on this experience, Herbst acknowledges that it was an important prelude to her study of Karl Marx, Friedrich Engels, Rosa Luxemburg, and other socialist thinkers, to her travels throughout America and Europe reporting on revolutionary situations, and to her decision to record in her fiction the impact of social and economic conditions on working-class people. But even at the start of this new era in her life, she says, she was certain that whatever she happened to do she would not act out of compulsive obedience to any political or artistic directives. Too much was at issue; she would respond to the pressures of history but she would not surrender her critical faculties.

1930s Journalism

Throughout the period that extended from the conclusion of her trip to Russia in 1930 to the end of her stay in Spain in 1937, Herbst strove to keep faith with the decision she made in Kharkov to confront contemporary history actively and honestly by carrying out with determination and competence the duties of a reporter. In this respect her journalism serves as a complement to her memoirs.

In her most significant journalism, written for such varied publications as the *New York Post* and the *New Masses*, she covered agrarian protest in the Midwest, revolutionary events in Cuba, the underground opposition to Hitler's *reich* in Germany, and the Spanish Civil War. Always on "special assignment," it was her job to get at the core of unrest not by giving an overview of the events but by presenting what average people involved in those events felt and thought. Well suited to her interests and temperament, these tasks gave her the opportunity to learn about social and political crises in the way she most valued: through firsthand contact with people whose commitments were directed more by personal need than by ideological conviction. They also allowed her to address constantly her most pressing concerns: economic reform and human rights.

Leftist ideas drawn from Marxism provide the basis for the sociopolitical criticism and observation that Herbst offers in her journalism. Her articles stress the oppression of the common people by existing economic and political institutions and suggest that such oppression can best be alleviated by changes that point toward the evolution of a socialistic society. Formally, the articles are a blend of essential factual information and of capsule sketches illustrating the human consequences of those facts; as such, they reflect the character of much documentary reporting of the times, when journalists attempted to evoke both intellectual and emotional responses in their audience.

Herbst's articles on farmers trace in microcosm the rise and decline of revolutionary sentiments in rural America during the first half of the 1930s. Published in *Scribner's Magazine*, "Feet in the Grass Roots" (1933) describes the Farmers' Holiday strike held in Sioux City during the summer of 1932 when about one thousand irate farmers and milk producers, protesting low prices for their products, picketed all roads leading to the city, turned away food trucks by the hundreds, and spilled milk into ditches or distributed it free. As presented in her report, the strikers see their action as part of an historic American tradition; they nickname the highway they are blocking "Bunker Hill 20," and liken their refusal to let farm products be delivered to market to the behavior of members of the Boston Tea Party. To augment the reader's sympathies for the striking farmers, Herbst shows they have grievances that thoroughly justify the action they have undertaken. She points out, in fact, that although these farmers have been faced with economic difficulties for many years, until recently each individual stoically shouldered his own burden. Now, with prices dropping far below the cost of production and with mortgage and interest rates climbing, their attitude has changed and they wish to publicize their problems and win support for their requests for an increase in prices and a moratorium on their debts. In closing, she notes that the protest has been suspended but wonders where and when the farmers' indignation will flare up again.

Her next article, "The Farmers Form a United Front" (1934), followed a troubled route to publication since it appeared in *New Masses* after having been rejected by the *New Republic*, most probably because its open criticism of the Roosevelt Administration did not quite conform to the position adopted by the editors, who at that time were disappointed by the New Deal but not ready to repudiate it.[4] In the article she tells how the delegates at the Farmers Second National Conference, which convened in Chicago in November, 1933, denounced the ineffectiveness of the measures adopted by President Roosevelt to help debt-burdened farmers by scaling down their mortgage and interest payments and to deal with the crucial problem of depressed prices and mounting surpluses by limiting the amount of land under cultivation. Further angered by their struggles with drought, they voted to demand cash relief and cancellation of their debts. To Herbst, they seemed determined to start an organized radical agrarian movement. Such a movement, however, never took shape, for the deadly drought which had begun in 1932 and continued each year until 1936, converting a huge area from the Dakotas to Texas into a Dust Bowl, transformed the dominant mood of the farmers from rebellion to desperation. Herbst discusses this change of attitude in "The Farmer Looks Ahead" (1935), written for the *American Mercury* after a trip through several drought-ridden states in the Midwest during which she had traveled many miles over land void of vegetation and had listened to tale after tale of eviction, hunger, and despair. Dissenting from some other reports that pictured the agrarian population of the upper Midwest as heroically enduring disaster, she emphasizes the farm families' desperation over still-declining prices for their products, their pain at taking relief checks, their bewilderment at a credit system that excluded the neediest of them, and especially their anguish at the knowledge that "for the first time in the history of this country there is no escaping to a fresh valley on the other side of the hill."[5]

In 1935, as the passions and energies of radical intellectuals in the United States began to be directed toward the international struggle against Fascism, Herbst started to report on unrest abroad. In March of that year she was commissioned by *New Masses* to write about the general strike in Cuba and to try to contact leaders of the insurrection. In "Cuba—Sick For Freedom" (1935) she explains that the key issues behind the strike were "bread and freedom"; the Depression was having disastrous effects on the price of sugar, the center of the island's economy, and the recently installed military junta headed by Fulgencio Batista, instead of proposing agrarian reforms, had enacted a number of measures designed to curtail civil liberties. Her other articles, "The Soviet in Cuba" (1935) and "A Passport from Realengo 18" (1936), are about the soviet Realengo 18, a pocket of peasant resistance high in the mountains of Oriente province. Here peasants, whom she describes as convinced that their action was part not only of the Cuban people's struggle for self-determination but also of an international movement for civil rights and human dignity, were fighting valiantly to hold onto land rightfully theirs and to cultivate it, not with sugar cane but with whatever crops they saw fit. In spite of the fact that violent retaliation by the Batista regime was making any form of protest in Cuba difficult to sustain, in all of her articles Herbst voices her hope that the revolution has not been completely defeated: "A whole people have been demoralized but they continue to raise their heads. The students have a word, *Tangana*, meaning to make a big noise. . . . A big noise fills this island, even if under repressive measures it has become for the moment a whisper."[6]

Later in 1935, deeply concerned about Hitler's consolidation of power in Germany, the land she had come to know while it was trying to rebuild itself after World War I, Herbst sought and was given an assignment to travel there as a journalist for the *New York Post*. Her specific task was to investigate opposition to the Nazi regime. In "Behind the Swastika" (1935), a six-part series of *Post* articles later collected in pamphlet form, and in an article for the *Nation*, "The German Underground War: Anti-Nazi Feeling Rises" (1936), she reports on the decline of democracy and the violation of civil rights in Germany and documents how, despite severe censorship of all forms of communication, an underground opposition managed to circulate its ideas with tiny leaflets, illegally published newspapers, slogans hastily scrawled in public places, and word of mouth. Yet she expressed doubt that any internal effort could overthrow the Hitler regime. Institutionalized terror was its strongest weapon and it knew how to wield that weapon all too well. Perhaps, as various members of the underground observed to her, the answer lay in war: "Some . . . hope that the ever-widening circle of Hitler's enemies will give the opposition strength to rid Germany of Hitler even before a great war comes; others feel they can only get rid of Hitler in such a world cataclysm."[7]

Herbst's articles about the Spanish Civil War—"Spanish Village" (*Nation*, 1937), "Housekeeping Under Fire" (*Woman's Day*, 1937), "Evening in Spain" (*Fight Against War and Fascism*, 1937), and "Night Comes to the Valley" (*Direction*, 1938)—are primarily about the International Brigades and life in primitive villages suddenly thrust into a sophisticated international conflict. What she says in them is thoroughly consistent with what she was to write in her memoir "The Starched Blue Sky of Spain." In fact, here too she emphasizes the idealism and spirit of self-sacrifice motivating the soldiers and expresses her admiration for the courage and sense of community displayed by the Spanish peasants, all the while suggesting that her worst fear is that the vast human potential of these peo-

ple will be violently repressed and destroyed. For instance, remembering
some women who showed her a new baby and communicated in gesture and word their hopes for his future, she writes:

In black clothes, with hair brushed back from faces that have looked on
much death, in shapeless canvas shoes, they stood there so full of vigor and
spirit, affirming life, that I wonder where I shall ever see their like again.
As one searches for certain music heard once, so I know that I shall be looking for those faces, or their like, the rest of my life.[8]

Chapter Eight
Achievement

Introducing excerpts from Josephine Herbst's trilogy anthologized in *The American Writer and the Great Depression* (1966), Harvey Swados remarked:

Of all the imaginative and rebellious writers of the depression, Josephine Herbst . . . has perhaps been the most seriously underestimated and [was] surely the most actively adventurous. Like a legendary reporter, she had the knack of being in the significant place at the crucial moment, and of being on a footing of comradely equality with many of the most important figures of the day. With the exception of John Dos Passos, no other writer at work in the thirties had even attempted a fictional reconstruction of American life as sweeping and ambitious as Josephine Herbst's trilogy. . . . It is no wonder that the publication of her memoirs, on which she has been at work for some years, is eagerly awaited.[1]

In a biographical profile of Herbst that appeared in *Mother Jones* in 1981, Elinor Langer observed:

If anyone has captured the pattern of American history from the 1860s to the 1930s as well as she has in her trilogy, I have not read it; in no other memoirs that I know of are the political and literary dilemmas of the 1920s and '30s more artfully portrayed. . . .[2]

As Swados and Langer suggest, Herbst's reputation will probably always remain tied to the Depression decade and to its immediate prelude and aftermath. In those years she produced her major work of fiction, the trilogy about the Trexler-Wendel family, and offered in her sociopolitical articles fine examples of documentary reportage, the special kind of journalism developed by the Left in that period. Moreover, the problems and challenges facing committed writers between 1926 and 1942 figure prominently in her memoirs. Yet it should not be forgotten that her career spanned half a century, evolving organically out of her personal and social preoccupations even as it reflected some representative intellectual and artistic trends.

Her early novels, *Nothing Is Sacred* and *Money for Love*, suggest an indebtedness to Ernest Hemingway, whose work she admired, in the sense that in them she tries to show that an uncluttered style based on ordinary words and short sentences can be used to express complex feelings accurately and faithfully. Their subject matter and the vision they convey, however, are peculiar to her, having originated in her social observation and experience. These novels are suffused with the trauma of adjustment, with the psychic strain of adaptation that was part of many middle-class individuals' responses to the 1920s. The world view they express is pessimistic. Each character begins his or her story in an intolerable situation and is later shown flirting with the possibility of release from it; but the attempt to escape is illusory and each ends in despair or resignation. The forces of society and the characters' own weaknesses, the author suggests, cannot be overcome.

In much the same manner as such contemporary works as John Dos Passos's *U. S. A.*, John Steinbeck's *The Grapes of Wrath*, and Ernest Hemingway's *For Whom The Bell Tolls*, her 1930s trilogy invites the reader to learn from history as well as fiction. Social and economic injustice, the development of the union movement and of radicalism, the Reconstruction, World War I, the stock market crash, the Depression, and the New Deal are some of the subjects on which it is centered; its major theme is the relationship of the individual to history. The historical scope expands as the trilogy progresses. After dramatizing the effects of American history from 1868 to 1914 on one troubled family in *Pity Is Not Enough*, Herbst studies what happened to average citizens in a troubled nation between 1914 and 1929 in *The Executioner Waits*, then covers significant economic and political disasters of a troubled world during the Depression in *Rope of Gold*. Her approach to history in these three volumes is autobiographically informed and parallels the evolution of certain radical ideas of the 1930s. The first volume, conceived of after she had decided to become socially engaged but before she entered her most radical phase, retains some of the pessimism expressed in her first two novels in its emphasis on victimization by history; the second book, clearly written under the ideological influence of Marxism during the period when she subscribed most fully to the shared ideals and goals of American radicalism, implies that organized protest may turn history around; in the third, which she worked on while and after being disappointed by the radical movement in the United States and abroad, efforts to influence the future are depicted as being seriously impeded by the burden of personal and national pasts. Reflecting her most deeply felt responses to the events of the Depression, each volume of her trilogy is characterized by a particular combination of anger and compassion—anger against the social, economic, and political institutions that waste human resources; compassion for the victims, who are sometimes also the agents, of those institutions. In all three the author writes with an element of didacticism but typically refuses to descend into dogmatism, making it clear throughout that while she feels that some major human problems could be solved by a radical reformation of society, she recognizes that no social transformation can alleviate all forms of human unhappiness. Furthermore, as is the case with the better political fiction of every period, in this work she is not concerned exclusively with social and economic issues but also develops with equal care such "private" subjects and themes as the bonds and tensions between parents and children and among siblings, initiation into a morally ambiguous world, falling in and out of love, facing ethical choices, dealing with frustration, human solidarity, loneliness, and death—topics of concern to her in all her work.

The start of the 1940s marked the end of an era in social and political history and the beginning of the decline of a literary generation, especially of those writers like John Dos Passos and James T. Farrell, who had directed their efforts toward social fiction. Herbst's career in the 1940s reflects these trends. Her novels from that period are existentially oriented, emphasizing problems relating to the inner being. *Satan's Sergeants* focuses explicitly on the effects of private guilt; in *Somewhere the Tempest Fell* the social and political crises discussed are less absorbing than the author's investigation of the fragmented selves of her characters. Whether out of specific autobiographical motives or a generally grave outlook on human nature, each of these novels expresses bitter poignancy at losses never to be recovered. Finally, both books are less successful artistically than her 1930s trilogy, for reasons that include an inability to make her habitually numerous story lines cohere around a well-defined interpretation of society.

Instead of continuing to grapple with the immense difficulties involved in creating a new form of social fiction, in the 1950s Herbst channeled a revitalized narrative skill into a gracefully written novella with few social overtones and discussed American society in a book of nonfiction. In the novella "Hunter of Doves" she provides another vision, less despairing than in her earlier work, of individuals striving to break through to life and achieve their human potentiality; blending a newly complex poetic style with expertise in working with the short fiction form acquired during several decades of writing short stories, she reestablishes herself as a thoughtful and talented artist. Her biography, *New Green World*, is not only about the past but is also an admonition to the present. She argues in it that contemporary neglect of what John and William Bartram embodied in their lives and work, an integration of science and human culture, is one source of some important tensions that have been plaguing American life since the start of the nineteenth century, especially nature versus man, science versus poetry, and the machine versus the spirit.

The memoirs Herbst published in the 1960s are distinguished for their literary power and wise sociopolitical insight. The product of intense dedication to her craft and of patient blending of observations and reflections accumulated over the decades, these memoirs offer an informed, subjective vision of some important aspects of the years between 1926 and 1942, representing them as they appeared to and were experienced by her and as they exist in her memory. Herbst addresses these memoirs to her contemporaries and to a younger generation, reminding the one and instructing the other about the complexities of the period of which she speaks and suggesting that many of its central dilemmas have yet to be resolved. Of the intellectual and literary climate of the 1920s she has much to say that is laudatory in "A Year of Disgrace," but she also points out what she conceives to be the danger of divorcing artistic experimentation from concern about the social, economic, and political realities of the surrounding world. Similarly, while acknowledging that beneficial advances were made by American society during the 1920s, she stresses the sometimes overlooked political repression of that decade, which culminated so tragically in the execution of Sacco and Vanzetti. Her comments on the 1930s in "The Starched Blue Sky of Spain" emphasize the disheartening dénoument of that period's collectively shared revolutionary goals and expectations, but record as well the inspiration that social involvement and activism produced in many radical and liberal intellectuals and assert that the most significant battles in which they engaged were not over ephemeral ideological questions but about moral issues related to the fate of humanity. In "Yesterday's Road" she discusses her experiences in Washington in 1942, when she was fired from a job that involved preparation of anti-Nazi propaganda, not only as a disastrous end to a decade of committed participation but also, and ironically, as an affirmation of that commitment. For, she maintains, although she and other activists had made mistakes, it was the evolution of history and not their inherent folly or criminal intent that had made their reasoned protest later seem subversive. She then turns her attention to a trip she took to Russia in 1930 to illustrate through one specific example some of the human and social factors underlying the decision made by members of her generation to link radicalism and literature to a degree never before attempted in the United States.

Individually, Herbst's novels, stories, essays, biography, and memoirs can be read as chronicles of her times, each an attempt to come to an understanding of a particular moment in the development of modern society and of the state of human consciousness. Considered as a whole, these works chart the responses of one sensitive and intelligent observer to her world and record her continuous effort to communicate the meaning of human experience as she had discovered it to be.

Notes and References

Chapter One

1. "Feet in the Grass Roots," *Scribner's Magazine* 93 (January 1933):46.
2. "My Pennsylvania Dutch Home," *Tomorrow* 10 (June 1951):19.
3. Elinor Langer, *Josephine Herbst* (Boston: Atlantic-Little, Brown, 1984), pp. 55–58.
4. "Nathanael West," *Kenyon Review* 23 (Fall 1961):617–18.
5. "Yesterday's Road," *New American Review* 3 (April 1968):92–93.
6. "A Year of Disgrace," *Noble Savage* 3 (May 1961):130.
7. Ibid., p. 129.
8. Jay Martin, *Nathanael West: The Art of His Life* (New York: Farrar, Straus, Giroux, 1970), p. 140.
9. "Literature in the U. S. S. R.," *New Republic* 66 (April 29, 1931):305.
10. In "Josephine Herbst," *Twentieth Century Authors*, ed. Stanley J. Kunitz and Howard Haycraft (New York: H. W. Wilson Co., 1942), p. 642.
11. Langer, *Josephine Herbst*, pp. 126–42.
12. In "Josephine Herbst," *Contemporary American Authors*, ed. Fred B. Millett (New York: Harcourt, Brace & World, 1940), p. 389.
13. Alfred Kazin, "Josephine Herbst (1897–1969)," *New York Review of Books*, March 27, 1969, p. 19.
14. "Spain's Agony: A Period of Exposure," *Nation* 203 (July 25, 1966):92.
15. "Yesterday's Road," p. 85.
16. Langer, *Josephine Herbst*, p. 259.
17. Allen Weinstein, *Perjury: The Hiss-Chambers Case* (New York: Knopf, 1978), pp. 137–42; Langer, *Josephine Herbst*, pp. 268–76.
18. Langer, *Josephine Herbst*, pp. 286–90.
19. In "Josephine Herbst," *Twentieth Century Authors: First Supplement*, ed. Stanley J. Kunitz and Vinta Colby (New York: H. W. Wilson Co., 1955), p. 438.
20. Langer, *Josephine Herbst*, pp. 277–82.
21. Kazin, "Josephine Herbst (1897–1969)," p. 19.

Chapter Two

1. "Ubiquitous Critics and the Author," *Newberry Library Bulletin* 5 (December 1958):3.

2. "Accomplishments," an unpublished memoir, The Collection of American Literature, Beinecke Rare Book and Manuscript Library, Yale University, p. 2.

3. "The Ruins of Memory," *Nation* 182 (April 14, 1956):304.

4. "Edward Dahlberg's *Because I Was Flesh*," *Southern Review* 1 (April 1965):341.

5. "Communism and the American Writer: A Report on the Tenth Newberry Library Conference on American Studies," *Newberry Library Bulletin* 5 (August 1959):103.

6. "The Ruins of Memory," p. 302.

7. "Accomplishments," p. 3.

Chapter Three

1. "Iowa Takes to Literature," *American Mercury* 7 (April 1926):466–70.

2. "A Year of Disgrace," *Noble Savage* 3 (May 1961):128–60.

3. *Nothing Is Sacred* (New York, 1928), p. 23; subsequent page references to this work given in the text in parentheses.

4. Clifton P. Fadiman, "Fiction Shorts," *Nation* 127 (October 24, 1928):432.

5. Ford Madox Ford, "A Distinguished First Novel," *Bookman* 68 (September 1928):87–88.

6. *New York Times Book Review,* October 21, 1928, p. 6.

7. T. S. Matthews, "American Particles," *New Republic* 57 (November 21, 1928):24–25.

8. Katherine Anne Porter, "The Family," *New York Herald Tribune-Books,* October 7, 1928, p. 2.

9. Katherine Anne Porter, "Bohemian Futility," *New Masses* 5 (November 1929):17–18.

10. *Saturday Review of Literature* 6 (October 19, 1929):298.

11. Florence Haxton, "Up in Harriet's Room," *New York Herald Tribune-Books,* October 6, 1929, pp. 5–6.

12. Isidor Schneider, "The Fetish of Simplicity," *Nation* 132 (February 18, 1931):184–86.

13. "Counterblast," *Nation* 132 (March 11, 1931):275–76.

Chapter Four

1. "Yesterday's Road," p. 103.

2. "The Ruins of Memory, p. 302.

3. In "Josephine Herbst," *Twentieth Century Authors* (New York, 1942), p. 641.

4. Walter B. Rideout, *The Radical Novel in the United States, 1900–1954* (Cambridge, Mass., 1956), p. 190.

5. *Pity Is Not Enough* (New York, 1933), p. 309; subsequent page references to this work given in the text in parentheses.

6. Basil Davenport, "Pity 'Tis True, 'Tis True," *Saturday Review of Literature* 9 (June 1933):629.

7. Horace Gregory, "Wealth in Shining Dollars," *New York Herald Tribune-Books*, May 28, 1933, p. 4.

8. Granville Hicks, "New Attitudes," *New Masses* 8 (June 1933):27.

9. "Authors' Field Day: A Symposium on Marxist Criticism," *New Masses* 12 (July 3, 1934):30.

10. *The Executioner Waits* (New York, 1934), p. 371.

11. Geoffrey Stone, "Thirteen Novels," *Commonweal* 21 (January 4, 1935):294–98.

12. Lionel Abel, "A Technician of Mediocrity," *Nation* 139 (October 31, 1934):513–16.

13. Mary Heaton Vorse, "What Happens to People," *New Republic* 81 (December 12, 1934):145–46.

14. Obed Brooks, "In the Great Tradition," *New Masses* 13 (November 27, 1934):22–23.

15. Edwin Berry Burgum, "A Significant Revolutionary Novel," *Partisan Review* 2 (January–February 1935):82–83.

16. Horace Gregory, "Josephine Herbst's Fresco of America," *New York Herald Tribune-Books*, October 28, 1934, p. 4.

17. Granville Hicks, *The Great Tradition* (New York: Macmillan, 1935), pp. 302–3.

18. *Rope of Gold* (New York, 1939), p. 397; subsequent page references to this work given in the text in parentheses.

19. Richard Cordell, "After the Gilded Age," *Saturday Review of Literature* 19 (March 4, 1939):7.

20. Philip Rhav, "A Variety of Fiction," *Partisan Review* 6 (Spring 1939):106–13.

21. Edwin Berry Burgum, "Josephine Herbst's *Rope of Gold*," *New Masses* 30 (March 21, 1939):22–24.

22. Alfred Kazin, "Flies in the Mid-West Kitchen," *New York Herald Tribune-Books*, March 5, 1939, p. 7.

23. Ibid.

24. Rideout, *The Radical Novel*, p. 245.

Chapter Five

1. "The Starched Blue Sky of Spain," *Noble Savage* 1 (March 1960):76–117.

2. "Yesterday's Road," pp. 84–104.

3. *Satan's Sergeants* (New York, 1941), p. 2; subsequent page references to this work given in the text in parentheses.

4. H. P. Lazarus, "In Solitary," *Nation* 152 (May 31, 1941):646.

5. Rose Feld, review of *Satan's Sergeants, New York Herald Tribune-Books,* May 4, 1941, p. 8.

6. *Somewhere the Tempest Fell* (New York, 1947), p. 317; subsequent page references to this work given in the text in parentheses.

7. Diana Trilling, "Fiction in Review," *Nation* 165 (December 13, 1947):653–54.

8. Howard Mumford Jones, "The Fallacy of 'Advanced' Fiction," *Saturday Review of Literature* 31 (February 28, 1948):15–16, 31–32.

9. Richard Sullivan, "Three Novels Shadowed by Mars," *New York Times Book Review,* November 23, 1947, p. 24.

Chapter Six

1. *New Green World* (New York, 1954), dustjacket; subsequent page references to this work given in the text in parentheses.

2. "Nathanael West," *Kenyon Review* 23 (Fall 1961):611.

3. Critics who have drawn on "Hunter of Doves" in their studies of Nathanael West include Randall Reid, *The Fiction of Nathanael West* (Chicago: University of Chicago Press, 1967) and Jay Martin, *Nathanael West: The Art of His Life* (New York: Farrar, Straus, & Giroux, 1970).

4. "Hunter of Doves," *Botteghe Oscure* 3 (Spring 1954):319; subsequent page references to this work given in the text in parentheses.

5. "Kept-Cat," *Occident* (University of California, Berkeley) 72 (October 1917):68; ibid. "Pagan" (November 1917), p. 125; "Star Dust" (April 1918), pp. 368–69; "Silences" (March 1918), pp. 317–18.

6. "The Elegant Mr. Gason," *Smart Set* 71 (July 1923):35–39; ibid., "Happy Birthday!" (November 1923), pp. 97–102.

7. "Dry Sunday in Connecticut," *American Mercury* 8 (July 1926):339–44.

8. "A Man of Steel," *American Mercury* 31 (January 1934):38.

9. "The Golden Egg," *Scribner's Magazine* 87 (May 1930):498.

10. "As A Fair Young Girl," *Scribner's Magazine* 88 (November 1930):513–19.

11. "The Last Word," *Tomorrow* 9 (September 1949):24.

12. "A Summer With Yorick," *Tomorrow* 8 (June 1949):31–36.

13. "A New Break," *Scribner's Magazine* 90 (September 1931):303–12; 326–44.

14. "I Hear You, Mr. and Mrs. Brown," *This Quarter* 3 (April–June 1931):709–20, reprinted in *Best American Short Stories of 1931 and The Yearbook of the American Short Story,* ed. Edward O'Brien (New York: Dodd, Mead & Co., 1931), pp. 179–89.

15. "The Governor Does Not Come," *Magazine: A Literary Journal* 1 (April 1934):157–60.

16. "The Golden Harvest," *Partisan Review and Anvil* 3 (March 1936):3–7.

17. "The Enemy," *Partisan Review* 3 (October 1936):7–12.

Chapter Seven

1. "A Year of Disgrace," *Noble Savage* 3 (May 1961):134; subsequent page references to this work given in the text in parentheses.

2. "The Starched Blue Sky of Spain," *Noble Savage* 1 (March 1960):79–80; subsequent page references to this work given in the text in parentheses.

3. "Yesterday's Road," *New American Review* 3 (April 1968):87; subsequent page references to this work given in the text in parentheses.

4. "The Farmers Form a United Front," *New Masses* 10 (January 2, 1934):20–23. Correspondence between Herbst and the editor of *The New Republic* appears at the end of the article.

5. "The Farmer Looks Ahead," *American Mercury* 34 (February 1934):212.

6. "Cuba—Sick For Freedom," *New Masses* 15 (April 2, 1935):18.

7. "The German Underground War: Anti-Nazi Feeling Rises," *Nation* 142 (January 8, 1936):42–43.

8. "Night Comes to the Valley," *Direction* 1 (April 1938):20.

Chapter Eight

1. Harvey Swados, *The American Writer and the Great Depression* (Indianapolis: Bobbs Merrill Co., 1966), pp. 103–4.

2. Elinor Langer, "If In Fact I Have Found A Heroine. . . . ," *Mother Jones* 6 (May 1981):37–46.

Selected Bibliography

PRIMARY SOURCES

1. Novels and Novella

Nothing Is Sacred. New York: Coward-McCann Co., 1928. Reprint. New York: Arno Press, 1977.

Money for Love. New York: Coward-McCann Co., 1929. Reprint. New York: Arno Press, 1977.

Pity Is Not Enough. New York: Harcourt, Brace & Co., 1933.

The Executioner Waits. New York: Harcourt, Brace & Co., 1934. Reprint. New York: AMS Press, 1977.

Rope of Gold. New York: Harcourt, Brace & Co., 1939. Reprint. New York: AMS Press, 1979.

Satan's Sergeants. New York: Charles Scribner's Sons, 1941.

Somewhere the Tempest Fell. New York: Charles Scribner's Sons, 1947.

"Hunter of Doves." *Botteghe Oscure* 3 (Spring, 1954): 310–44. A novella. Reprinted in *The Writer's Signature.* Edited by Elaine Gottlieb Hemley and Jack Matthews. Glenview, Ill.: Scott, Foresman & Co., 1972, pp. 107–138.

2. Biography

New Green World. New York: Hastings House, 1954; London: Weidenfeld & Nicolson, 1954.

3. Memoirs

"The Starched Blue Sky of Spain." *Noble Savage* 1 (March, 1960):76–117.

"A Year of Disgrace." *Noble Savage* 3 (May, 1961):128–60.

"Yesterday's Road." *New American Review* 3 (April, 1968):84–104. Reprinted in *Literature at the Barricades: The American Writer in the 1930s.* Edited by Ralph F. Bogardus and Fred Hobson. University, Ala.: University of Alabama Press, 1982, pp. 29–45.

4. Poems

"Kept-Cat." *Occident* (University of California, Berkeley) 72 (October 1917):68.

"Pagan." *Occident* 72 (November 1917):125.

"Silences." *Occident* 72 (March 1918):317–18.
"Star-Dust." *Occident* 72 (April 1918):368–69.

5. Short Stories

"The Elegant Mr. Gason," *Smart Set* 71 (July 1923):35–39. Under pseudonym Carlotta Greet.

"Happy Birthday!" *Smart Set* 71 (November 1923):97–102. Under pseudonym Carlotta Greet.

"Dry Sunday in Connecticut." *American Mercury* 8 (July 1926):339–44.

"Summer Boarders." *The Second American Caravan.* Edited by Alex Kreymborg, Louis Mumford, and Paul Rosenfeld. New York: Macaulay Company, 1928, pp. 536–45.

"Pennsylvania Idyl," *American Mercury* 16 (January 1929):52–59. With John Herrmann.

"Once A Year." *transition,* no. 16–17 (June 1929), pp. 94–104.

"The Golden Egg." *Scribner's Magazine* 87 (May 1930):492–99.

"A Bad Blow." *Scribner's Magazine* 88 (July 1930):25–32.

"Top of the Stairs." *American Mercury* 21 (October 1930):226–32.

"As A Fair Young Girl." *Scribner's Magazine* 88 (November 1930):513–19.

"I Hear You, Mr. and Mrs. Brown." *This Quarter* 3 (April-June 1931):709–20. Reprinted in *Best American Short Stories of 1931 and The Yearbook of the American Short Story.* Edited by Edward J. O'Brien. New York: Dodd, Mead & Co., 1931, pp. 179–89.

"A New Break." *Scribner's Magazine* 90 (September 1931):303–12, 326–44.

"A Dreadful Night." *Pagany* 3 (January–March 1932):119–24. Reprinted in *A Return to Pagany: The History, Correspondence and Selections from a Little Magazine, 1929–1933.* Edited by Stephen Halpert. Boston: Beacon Press, 1969, pp. 409–14.

"I Saw Your Light." *This Quarter* 5 (December 1932):304–18.

"A Very Successful Man." *American Mercury* 29 (June 1933):211–20.

"She Showed the Cloven Hoof." *Magazine: A Literary Journal* 1 (December 1933):7–11.

"A Man of Steel." *American Mercury* 31 (January 1934):32–40.

"The Governor Does Not Come." *Magazine: A Literary Journal* 1 (April 1934):157–60.

"You Can Live Forever." *Dubuque Dial,* no. 1 (June–December 1934), pp. 1–5.

"The Golden Harvest." *Partisan Review and Anvil* 3 (March 1936):3–7.

"The Enemy." *Partisan Review* 3 (October 1936):7–12.

"Embalmer's Holiday." *Accent* 1 (Winter 1941):85–93.

"Just Like a Ship." *New Yorker* 19 (January 1, 1944):40, 42.

"A Summer With Yorick." *Tomorrow* 8 (June 1949):31–36.

"The Last Word." *Tomorrow* 9 (September 1949):22–24.

"Leave Me Out of the Picture." *American Mercury* 83 (December 1956):63–68.

6. Sociopolitical Essays

"Lynching in the Quiet Manner." *New Masses* 7 (July 1931):11. Reprinted
in *Negro*. Edited by Nancy Cunard. London: Wishart & Co., 1934, pp.
269–71.

"Feet in the Grass Roots." *Scribner's Magazine* 93 (January 1933):46–51.
Reprinted as "The 1930's: Farmer's Holiday" in *Scribner's Magazine* 101
(January 1937):105–7 and as "Farmers' Holiday" in *Modern American
Vistas*. Edited by Howard W. Hintz and Bernard D. N. Grebanier.
New York: Dryden Press, 1940, pp. 107–19.

"Farmers Form a United Front." *New Masses* 10 (January 2, 1934):20–23.
Reprinted as "American Farmers Ride Into Action" in *Labour Monthly*
16 (February 1934):114–19.

"The Farmer Looks Ahead." *American Mercury* 34 (February 1935):212–19.

"The Soviet in Cuba." *New Masses* 14 (March 19, 1935):9–12.

"Cuba—Sick For Freedom." *New Masses* 15 (April 2, 1935):17–18.

"A Passport From Realengo 18." *New Masses* 16 (July 16, 1935):10–11.
Reprinted in *New Masses: An Anthology of the Rebel Thirties*. Edited by
Joseph North. New York: International Publishers, 1969, p. 155–59.

"Behind The Swastika." A series of six articles published in the *New York
Post* daily between October 28 and November 2, 1935. Reprinted as
pamphlet in 1935 by the Committee Against War and Fascism. Reprinted in *Press Time: A Book of Post Classics*. New York: Books, Inc.,
1936, pp. 335–41.

"The German Underground War: Anti-Nazi Feeling Rises." *Nation* 142
(January 8, 1936):41–43.

"Spanish Village." *Nation* 145 (August 14, 1937):167–70.

"Housekeeping Under Fire." *Woman's Day* 1 (October 7, 1937):16–17.

"Evening in Spain." *Fight Against War and Fascism* 5 (November 1937):13,
30.

"Night Comes to the Valley." *Direction* 1 (April 1938):18–20.

"Good Neighbors—Whose Grab Bag?" *Friday* (August 6, 1940), pp. 1–4.

7. Essays about Literature and Art

"Iowa Takes to Literature." *American Mercury* 7 (April 1926):466–70.

"Counterblast." *Nation* 132 (March 11, 1931):271–76.

"Literature in the U.S.S.R." *New Republic* 66 (April 29, 1931):305–6.

"Miss Porter and Miss Stein." *Partisan Review* 15 (May 1948):568–72.

"The Ruins of Memory." *Nation* 182 (April 14, 1956):302–4. Reprinted in
A View of The Nation: An Anthology. Edited by Henry M. Christman.
New York: Grove Press, 1960, pp. 19–25.

"Ubiquitous Critics and the Author." *Newberry Library Bulletin* 5 (December
1958):1–13.

"The Dial and Modern Art." *Arts Magazine* 33 (September 1959):26–33.

"Nathanael West." *Kenyon Review* 23 (Fall 1961):611–30. Reprinted in abbreviated form in *Twentieth Century Interpretations of Miss Lonelyhearts: A Collection of Critical Essays.* Edited by Thomas H. Jackson. Englewood Cliffs, N.J.: Prentice Hall, 1971, pp. 39–45, and in *The Writer's Signature,* Edited by Elaine Gottlieb Hemley and Jack Matthews. Glenview, Ill.: Scott, Foresman and Co., 1972, pp. 139–52.

"Van Gogh Comprehensive." *Arts Magazine* 36 (December 1961):56–63.

"Only the Best" (review of Nicholas Joost, *Scofield Thayer and The Dial: An Illustrated History*). *Kenyon Review* 27 (Spring 1965):353–59.

"Edward Dahlberg's *Because I Was Flesh.*" *Southern Review* 1 (April 1965):337–51. Reprinted in *American Ishmael of Letters.* Edited by Harold Billings. Austin, Texas: Roger Beacham, 1968, pp. 95–105.

"Moralist's Progress" (review of Granville Hicks, *Part of the Truth: An Autobiography*). *Kenyon Review* 27 (Fall 1965):772–74.

"A Language Absolutely Unliterary." Introduction to *Gullible's Travels by Ring Lardner.* Chicago: University of Chicago Press, 1965. pp. v–xv.

"Spain's Agony: A Period of Exposure." *Nation* 203 (July 25, 1966):91–94.

"Foreword" to *Journey Into Revolution: Petrograd 1917–18 by Albert Rhys Williams.* Edited by Lucita Williams. Chicago: Quadrangle Books, 1969, pp. 9–16.

8. Miscellaneous

"Farewell and a Promise to Barbusse." *New Masses* 17 (October 1, 1935):11–12.

"Bucks County Auction." *Vogue's First Reader.* Edited by Frank Crowninshield. New York: Julian Messner, 1942, pp. 347–51.

"Josephine Herbst Tells Why She Was Fired from the COI." *PM,* June 17, 1942.

"My Pennsylvania Dutch Home." *Tomorrow* 10 (June 1951):18–21.

"Bucks County, Pennsylvania: A Country Place for City People." *Commentary* 28 (December 1959):515–20.

9. Manuscripts

Josephine Herbst's papers, which include journals, manuscripts, and photographs, as well as extensive personal correspondence and a typed copy of her first, unpublished novel, "Following the Circle," are in the Collection of American Literature, The Beinecke Rare Book and Manuscript Library, Yale University.

Several letters, a copy of "Behind the Swastika," and a corrected typescript of *Somewhere The Tempest Fell* are in the Iowa Authors Collection, the University of Iowa Library, Iowa City, Iowa.

SECONDARY SOURCES

1. Bibliography

Pickering, Martha Elizabeth. "A Biography and Checklist of Josephine
   Herbst." 1968. Unpublished. Copy obtained from Eakins Press, New
   York. Copy in the Collection of American Literature, Beinecke Rare
   Book and Manuscript Library, Yale University.

2. Biography and General Criticism

Andrews, Clarence A. *A Literary History of Iowa.* Iowa City: University of
   Iowa Press, 1972.

Although Andrews offers very few comments on Herbst's fiction, he observes
   that "she may well be the best novelist Iowa has turned out."

Authors' Field Day: A Symposium on Marxist Criticism. *New Masses* 12
   (July 3, 1934):27–32.

One of fourteen authors who commented on the literary criticism in *New
   Masses,* Herbst said that she found it to be vague, dogmatic, and patronizing, and took Granville Hicks to task for failing to see that *Pity
   Is Not Enough,* in dealing with the decline of rugged individualism, was
   a novel not only about the past but also addressed to the present.

Betsky, Celia. "Reconsideration: The Trilogy of Josephine Herbst." *New
   Republic* 179 (July 8 and 15, 1978):45–46.

A brief, perceptive assessment of how Herbst's conception of history, her
   experiences in the 1930s, and her awareness of the relationships and
   tensions between the personal and the political shaped *Pity Is Not
   Enough, The Executioner Waits,* and *Rope of Gold,* "three extraordinary
   works of great beauty and great strength."

Bevilacqua, Winifred Farrant. "An Introduction to Josephine Herbst,
   Novelist." *Books at Iowa,* no. 25 (November 1976), pp. 1–19.

Discusses the major themes and literary techniques of Herbst's novels.

————. "The Novels of Josephine Herbst." Ph.D. diss. University of Iowa,
   1977.

Offers a brief biography of the author, then evaluates her seven novels, giving special emphasis to her social observation and critique and to the
   development of her craft. The concluding chapter draws on her critical
   essays, her memoirs, and her journalism to discuss how Herbst's responses to the literary movements and the social and political events of
   her times helped shape her career.

Craig, Robert L. "The Social and Political Journalism of Josephine
   Herbst." M. A. thesis, University of Iowa, 1978.

In this interesting descriptive analysis of Herbst's sociopolitical articles,
   Craig argues that she wrote as a nondogmatic Marxist and as a documentary journalist in the tradition of the 1930s.

Gourlie, John M. "The Evolution of Form in the Works of Josephine Herbst." Ph.D. diss. New York University, 1975.
Examining the narrative techniques in Herbst's unpublished manuscript "Following the Circle," her seven novels, and her novella "Hunter of Doves," Gourlie discerns in the development of her literary form two distinct phases. The first phase begins in the 1920s, with works that show her gaining mastery of a decentralized form, and reaches its summit in the broad panorama of her 1930s "collective" trilogy. The second includes her novels of the 1940s, which show her narrowing the focus of her fiction, and has its climax in the tightly controlled narrative of "Hunter of Doves."

Guards Ousted Liberal Writer from COI Job. *PM,* June 15, 1942.
The fourth in a series of articles on "the 'Red' witch hunt now being conducted by Federal agencies among liberals in public service and in certain war industries," this piece describes the circumstances of Herbst's firing from her job in Washington.

Hardwick, Elizabeth. "Introduction" to Josephine Herbst, *Nothing Is Sacred.* New York: Arno Press, 1977. (Rediscovered Fiction by American Women Series).
Praises Herbst's precise, economic style and the way she captures the essence of her characters' mundane lives.

————. "Introduction" to Josephine Herbst, *Money for Love.* New York: Arno Press, 1977. (Rediscovered Fiction by American Women Series).
Offers brief comments on "the bold social and moral accuracy" with which Herbst delineates her hopelessly provincial characters.

Kazin, Alfred. "Josephine Herbst (1897–1969)." *New York Review of Books,* March 27, 1969, pp. 19–20.
A tender memorial eulogy.

Kempthorne, Dion Quintin. "Josephine Herbst: A Critical Introduction." Ph.D. diss. University of Wisconsin, 1973.
After a biographical chapter which details the facts of Herbst's life and briefly discusses some of her short stories to show how she incorporated autobiographical material into her work, Kempthorne examines her seven novels, her novella "Hunter of Doves," and her biography *New Green World.* The novels are considered in light of the predominant literary trends of the decades in which they were written and explicated to trace the evolution of one of Herbst's overriding themes: the desire for freedom. "Hunter of Doves" is seen as highly imaginative literary criticism and *New Green World* as an expression of her interest in ecology.

Langer, Elinor. *Josephine Herbst.* Boston: Atlantic-Little, Brown and Company, 1984.
Making skillful use of Herbst's extensive correspondence and of her journals, as well as of information gathered in conversations with many of her

friends and associates, Langer presents a dramatically revealing portrait of Herbst as a passionate, courageous, and complex woman. Her biography also illuminates various facets of American history in the twentieth century since her depiction of Herbst's private life and of her radical activism are set against a perceptive re-creation of her times.

_____. "If In Fact I Have Found a Heroine . . ." *Mother Jones* 6 (May 1981):37–46.

A sensitive and stimulating introductory essay on Herbst's personal life, her career as a writer and journalist, and her sociopolitical ideas and activities.

Madden, David. *Proletarian Writers of the Thirties.* Carbondale: Southern Illinois University Press, 1968.

The "Introduction" to this collection of essays is in part a response to objections raised by Herbst in a letter in which she declined to contribute an essay for the volume on the grounds that the label "proletarian" was too narrow and arbitrary and had been "used more as blackmail than as a definitive term with any valid meaning." Quotes excerpts from her correspondence that describe her intentions in writing her trilogy.

Pratt, Annis. (with Barbara White, Andrea Loewenstein, and Mary Wyer). *Archetypal Patterns in Women's Fiction.* Bloomington, Indiana: Indiana University Press, 1981.

In a chapter on novels of social protest, Pratt includes a short analysis of "sexual politics" in Herbst's trilogy.

Rideout, Walter. "Forgotten Images of the Thirties: Josephine Herbst." *Literary Review* 27 (Fall 1983): 28–36.

After a summary of Herbst's life through the end of the 1930s, Rideout briefly discusses how her trilogy evokes both the despair and the hopes of the Depression years.

_____. *The Radical Novel in the United States, 1900–1954: Some Interrelations of Literature and Society.* Cambridge: Harvard University Press, 1956.

Contains an excellent short study of Herbst's trilogy as an example of the kind of 1930s work that used the theme of the revolutionary development of some characters as a contrast to the theme of the distintegration of the middle class. Places her trilogy, along with Nelson Algren's *Somebody in Boots* and James T. Farrell's Studs Lonigan trilogy, among "the most durable achievements of the radical novel of the thirties."

Schneider, Isidor. "The Fetish of Simplicity." *Nation* 132 (February 18, 1931):184–86.

Cites Herbst as "a writer with definite narrative gifts" but who in her novels *Nothing Is Sacred* and *Money For Love* did not realize to the full her literary powers because she succumbed to the unfortunate effects of the self-consciously bare and simple writing of the "Hemingway school."

Herbst replied in "Counterblast," *Nation* 132 (March 11, 1931):275–76.

T. R. B. "Washington Notes: America's Gestapo." *New Republic* 106 (June 15, 1942):88.

A sympathetic account of Herbst's dismissal from employment at the German desk of the Donovan Committee in Washington, D.C.

What Is Americanism: A Symposium on Marxism and the American Tradition. *Partisan Review and Anvil* 3 (April 1936):3–18.

Herbst was one of ten writers who responded to questions about the relationship between the American tradition and Marxism. Her reply, which includes a short history of her family, expresses her belief that some aspects of Marxism should be incorporated into American society and asserts that the dream of having a better, more dignified life is not uniquely American but is shared throughout the world.

Index